Pass Christi Historic District

The Author – Dan Ellis
Until Hurricane Katrina, resided at:
Pass Christian, MS

Now resides at:
Eureka Springs, AR

email: DanEllis@DanEllis.Net
Web Site – www.danellis.net

First Release: December 1999 – Limited Color Edition
Second Release: July 2000 – Black & White Edition
Minor revisions for Internet distributions – May 2011

Dedication

This reprinted book is dedicated to all the Katrina Survivors
who chose to sweat out the slow processes of Recovery
and the heartbreaking turmoil
of remaining in Pass Christian
and who individually struggled to
bring it back, all the while,
remembering Paradise.

Dan Ellis -- *Community Historicizer*

Dan Ellis's presentation of historic facts is unique in its format. Historic data is arranged into chronological categories and themes complete with photographs, maps, and interviews. A reader can pick up one of his books and start reading from any page, because each segment is a different story. He says that he derived this format from when he was a history teacher and taught his students to learn how each episode in life is a separate story. His first meaningful book was written as a highschool teacher when requested by the school system to teach a course in "Americanism vs Communism." At that time, there was no text book, so he had to do the research and write the book.

As a pioneer in the early days of computers, Ellis was a principal in a company that sold time and services on a very large computer system. As his customers began installing their own computers, they would induce his computer operators and programmers to join their staff. This opened a new door for him. He began training entry level personnel to fill computer positions in local businesses, hospitals, banks, and government facilities. In this endeavor, there were no text books, so Ellis created the training manuals and supplied documentation for software programs. With the introduction of personal computers in the early 80s, Ellis once more took the challenge and revised his old text manuals to conform to training eager,

novice professionals seeking to initiate their own computers.

In 1990, Ellis established permanent residence at his Pass Christian weekend home. His interest in writing lead to publishing vignette columns in local newspapers. Upon writing his first histories, he realized a significant amount of misinformation abounded. This resulted in his seeking primary source information from archival records in Mobile, Alabama, Jackson, Mississippi, New Orleans, Louisiana, and from local court houses and churches.

Ellis's books are filled with treasured photographs and maps; and he takes special effort to seek out individuals, whether obscure or prominent — those who can add a touch of personal experience by revealing anecdotal interviews.

Not being able to find a publisher, Ellis was determined to get his history books to the general public, so he learned to be a self-publisher and now distributes his history books through bookstores and gift shops. His first published book was on Diamondhead followed by Pass Christian, Bay St. Louis/Hancock, Gulfport Centennial, Kiln Kountry, and Gulf Coast Panorama. He is looking forward to writing the histories of those towns that do not have updated history books, such as D'Iberville, Ocean Springs, and Pascagoula in Mississippi and the West Florida parishes in Louisiana.

Ellis's books are computerized in order to enable easy updating and error corrections. He calls himself an *Historiographer and Scrutinier*, which simply translates to a "writer of history with authenticity."

Dan Ellis can be reached at: www.danellis.net

The Cover

The Dixie White House that was located at Scenic Drive and Lang Avenue was demolished following heavy damages by Hurricane Camille in August 1969.

The Book

The first trial publication was printed with only two copies being made, one to the Pass Christian Historical Society, and one for "pass around" review. Because of so many requests for a permanent issue, this book was updated and informative chapters have been added.

The Contents

Historical Background
Early Cottage construction
Heritage Organizations
Live Oak Trees
Castles in the Sand
Early Hotels
Lost Forever

Decimation of Homes
Vanished Mansions
Historic District Tour Guide
Registered homes and buildings
Katrina affects and more
Architectural Glossary

Davis Avenue view from Scenic Drive - early 1900s

All of the buildings in this photograph of Davis Avenue are lost forever.
The building at the right, is the Mexican Gulf Hotel which burned down in 1917.

Dedication

In Memoriam

Without doubt, this book would not have been possible had it not been for the record files and photographs in the ***"Billy Bourdin Historical Collection."*** When Billy finds a responsive person in the community, he is most formidable in his support of promoting and sharing his heritage and data files. Further, Billy's retention for names and event happenings makes the community's heritage come alive.

Through the years, his collection of photographs have extended past the walls of his plumbing shop and are encased in large albums. Besides maintaining a storage for all of the original source material, including nearly a century of editions of past local newspapers, magazines, periodicals and anything else printed about the Pass, he has studiously made selective xerox copies that he has clipped, sorted, and compiled into almost 500 categories of chronological events and personalities that have been significant to Pass Christian's heritage. Each file of information is studiously maintained and upgraded in separate folders with protective plastic page shields and stored in large file drawers with a system that would make a librarian proud.

Not a person, local resident or out-of-town visitor, has ever left his place without having been well impressed and more informed. The following recent commentary speaks for all of us who knew Billy Bourdin!

"During a recent, unexpected visit to Pass Christian, Mississippi, my husband and I encountered an amazing local historian, Mr. Billy Bourdin, who has spent decades collecting the stories of his area. He has personally photographed and collected photographs and information about hundreds of houses and buildings in Pass Christian, a quaint village on the Gulf of Mexico and has, as well, researched the lives of the inhabitants. All this he does for the love of gathering history. His office is a veritable museum which should be appreciated by all lovers of knowledge about the past"

Thank you Billy, from all who know you and appreciate the time, patience, and cost that it takes to maintain such an undertaking that you have been challenged by!

Welcome to the Golden Gulf Coast!
Welcome to the Antebellum homes of the Pass!

Pass Christian, pronounced Christi-anne, was founded in 1699 by French-Canadians d'Iberville and Bienville. As more explorations took place along the Coast, in 1748, Nicholas Christian d'Ladnier established his home and cattle farm at Cat Island. It was his name, that was conferred on the peninsular village and the channel that lays before it, of which both are known as *Pass Christian.*

During the early 1800s, the *Pass* was visited by schooners plying the Gulf of Mexico from New Orleans to Mobile. Pass Christian was one of the favorite *watering holes* that had a large grandiose hotel fronting on the beach. The famous and magnificent *Pass Christian Hotel* was ensconced in the mid-1830s.

Shortly afterwards, appeared the *Mansion House,* the *Sans Souci,* the *St. Nicholas House* (which was exclusively for bachelors), the *Napoleon Hotel,* and the *Crescent Hotel.* In addition, there were several boarding houses and private homes that also accommodated guests.

It was at the Pass Christian Hotel that the *Southern Regatta Club* was formed in 1849, which was the precursor to the Southern Yacht Club and the Pass Christian Yacht Club. Hotel guests were entertained by attending gala balls, musical diversions, moonlight sailboat rides, beach parties, and carriage drives through the piney woods. Seafood and Creole dishes were prepared regularly in addition to specialty recipes brought in from visiting tourists from Europe. The Yacht Club became a Mecca for sailing enthusiasts. Voyages at sunset or by moonlight along the magnificent coastline, or to the nearby islands, created a constant parade of billowing sails.

Former coast historian, Ray Thompson, described that, "Long before Pascagoula, Ocean Springs, Mississippi City (now, part of Gulfport) or Biloxi had hit their stride entertaining coast visitors, this community of Pass Christian was an old established and favorite summer retreat for the cotton and cane planters of Alabama, Mississippi and Louisiana. These planters were the first to build private cottages and second home villas along the four mile stretch of (shell) roadway that fronted the beach area of Pass Christian."

Year round commuter service with reliable, inexpensive steamboat connections between New Orleans and Pass Christian encouraged many Orleanians to build homes, resulting in dual citizenship for many.

Spreading out from the center of the early village of Pass Christian, fronting the beaches, wealthy people from New Orleans and nearby plantations erected a multitude of cottages. As time passed, each owner attempted to outdo the other in architectural performance. This new inflow of residents clamored for relaxation and recreation befitting the royalty of the "*Champs Elysees*". It was even more advantageous for those who could compress their work week and extend their weekends.

The *Pass* achieved great fame as a summer resort. Loyal patrons were the Mississippi Plantation owners and the financial barons from New Orleans. A colony of true aristocracy was born during this era. Visitors also arrived from other states to enjoy the cool Gulf breezes, the refreshing waters, and the sophisticated elegance offered only in Pass Christian. Returning visitors spoke frequently of the attractiveness of the *Pass*.

It was these beginnings that in the 1830s, Pass Christian evolved into a thriving community. This was largely due to its proximity to New Orleans and its participation as a "sister city" in culture as well as in its dynamic spirit. Its first mercantile activity was that of a trading center. The *Pass* had developed as a small port for local fishermen and arriving boats passing through to other port communities along the Coast between Mobile and New Orleans.

In 1839, the post office was established. In 1844, the first Catholic Mission Church was built and in 1851, it was replaced with a larger church that was mounted with a high steeple. In the mean time, other faithful Christians had built the Trinity Episcopal Church in 1849.

The Town of Pass Christian was incorporated on February 21st, 1848.

During the summer of 1847, a reporting from the *"Daily Delta"* of New Orleans, stated, "There are a good number of private residences and villas there, and many staid and solemn people who are perfectly satisfied to sit in their balconies, to smoke their Victorias, curse their appetites, and play out in their imaginations numerous little fishing parties."

During 1849 and 1850, a renaissance of architectural structures were built along the beach front of Pass Christian. Wealthy planters and brokers vied with each other in building antebellum mansions of great splendor. Sixty such homes were built during that period alone. It was also during this period that some of the residents started making their own wines from the grape orchards that they cultivated. By 1860, Pass Christian was recognized as the Queen City of the Mississippi Gulf Coast.

Numerous piers and wharfs were built, extending out from the shore embankments into the Mississippi Sound. These stretched along the coast for approximately a mile on each side of the center of town. The boat wharfs were built high atop pilings. The oldest location was the Lighthouse wharf, protruding out from the beach in front of the present day City Hall at Heirn Street where the Pass Christian lighthouse had been erected in 1831. That wharf primarily provided docking for the passenger boats arriving from Mobile and New Orleans, which was just a block from the Pass Christian Hotel and a short walk to the Crescent Hotel, later the Harbour Inn Bed and Breakfast.

Quoting from Dr. J.J. Hayden, "each cottage maintained an accompanying private wharf extending out into the Gulf. A pier was built on pilings with a bath house structured at its furthest end into the Sound. Bathing hours were established for the ladies at an appointed hour, and another specified time for gentlemen."

"At the established woman's bathing hour, one can vision the ladies, young and old, tripping out to the bath-houses. It was customary to be draped in long flowing apparel with their heads and faces discreetly veiled or hooded. At the end of the pier they would disrobe and descend into the cool Gulf waters and dig their toes into the white sand bottoms while wading and washing," reported Hayden.

In 1860, the population for Harrison County was 5000 in addition to 1000 slaves, and Pass Christian was known as the Queen City of the Mississippi Gulf Coast. At that time, a continuing stream of immigrants and adventurers from the Carolinas and Georgia were settling the Gulf seaboard.

With the building of the New Orleans, Mobile and Chattanooga Railroad in 1869, Pass Christian opened its doors to become the winter resort for northerners seeking to escape the cold. Store fronts and services were established to care for the local residents as well as the frequent visitors.

Before the Civil War, the *Pass* was the largest trading center in Harrison County, exporting many stores and supplies to other world markets. Mississippi pine and cypress timber forests were cut and exported. Throughout the piney woods, kilns were built to produce large quantities of tar and charcoal.

These products were brought by ox-cart to the *Pass* either for local consumption or loaded on ships for export to New Orleans or other destinations. Pass Christian also developed as a sheep and wool center, with sheep herders bringing their stock to local auctions for shearing and export. At that time, all roads led to Pass Christian. The Rhodes store, now the VFW hall at Scenic Drive, was where the sheep owners sold their wool to the highest bidders. With the money, the sheep men bought provisions, food, and clothing to take back home with them.

In 1897, tracks were laid along the beachfront from Biloxi to Pass Christian in providing local and tourist traffic to travel by street-car while viewing the beauty of the Mississippi Sound. In 1904, mule power was substituted by electric power. However, since the Beach Avenue residents of the *Pass* refused obstructions on their beaches, the tracks were diverted to Second Street and stopped at Trinity Church. This mode of travel ended in the late 1920s as automobiles made their emergence.

Some of the residents had started cultivation and even produced their own wines from their cultured grape orchards. One of these men, Alfred Davis, became a well known wine producer from his scuppernong grapes.

Before the turn of the century, in 1895, Roderic McIntosh, was a saloon-keeper who was considered a connoisseur of liquors and cigars.

He owned and named his tavern *The Sazerac* after the famed "Sazerac Saloon" in New Orleans – and he was proud to equal its quality of drinks and service. The McIntosh tavern was located on First Street (now Scenic Drive) during the 1880s.

The Sazerac in Pass Christian was a great success because it maintained a large inventory of imported wines, liqueurs, cordials, and choice liquors from all over. The bar-keep also served the famed local Scuppernong Wine produced by Colonel Davis' winery.

This lifestyle lasted for better than a hundred years. It was a way of life that thrived on luxury, peacefulness, and graciousness. The daily sentiment was calm, tranquil, and with a closeness of family, . . . and, a lifestyle that is still apparent today.

This is where the livin' is easy. Where tea and mint juleps are specially proffered only to personal friends of choice. Where the enchantment of plantation life is manifested in modified but continued glory. Where a persevering spirit for past heritage is mandated and upheld as inviolate. Where even the former newcomers and outsiders have adapted proudly to original Southern Traditions.

There are more individual homes along the full extent of the Pass Christian Historic District which are listed in the National Registry, than any other community along the Coast. The original historic values of the *Pass* are subtly preserved from diminution and yet sustained in continued prominence. Many of the owners have "open house" during seasons of annual Home Tours and Pilgrimages, thereby bringing back memories of the *Pass* as *"Queen City of the Coast."*

Ballymere is recognized as one of the oldest cottages on Scenic Drive. There are numerous other beautiful structures that have survived time and hazardous storms, such as the former Crescent Hotel, now the Harbour Inn, and the Union Quarters mansion, both on Scenic Drive, which is still locally known as *Beach Boulevard.*

The *Pass,* citing from *The Gulf Coast of Mississippi*, Nola Nance Oliver states, that "God wafts the breath of this favored Southland to the frozen North to show them that summer lives. The thrifty inhabitants send the message northward in luscious fruits and fragrant blossoms that thrive all year on the Coast. Here the treasures of earth, sea and sky abound."

Pass Christian continues to be a place of interest in making news regionally as well as nationally. An August 1999 article in the <u>Orlando Sentinel</u>, by Heather McPherson, entitled *"Pass Christian, a gem amid the glitter,"* was reported.

"Travelers to this area are rediscovering a string of long-overlooked communities along U.S. Highway 90. Ocean Springs, Long Beach, Bay St. Louis, Waveland and Pass Christian. While each of the towns offers a distinct seaside splendor, Pass Christian is arguably the fairest of them all."

"Its beach front is lined with majestic magnolias and distinctive homes. Its inland area is laced with grassy, velvet hammock land and, in the spring, the azaleas leave broad brush strokes of hot pink blooms along the narrow streets and driveways. "The city is a three-dimensional showcase of Victorian and Creole-Caribbean architecture and design."

"Compared to Biloxi, where the clicking of the roulette wheels seem to set the beat a bit faster, Pass Christian is the place for travelers who prefer to experience their repasts in slow strides . . . it's the kind of place where the expression *sit and stay awhile* means something . . . and instills a *stop and smell the roses* attitude."

The *Pass* has its very own unique qualities. It is for this reason that so many have journeyed here to make their quest. The *Pass* is a weekend and summer resort as well as a residential community substantially inhabited by retirees from New Orleans and many other Southern communities including Midwestern and Northern states. A number of home owners access their dwellings only for week-ends or summer get-away facilities. The result, however, is that they unfortunately never penetrate past the facade. Only in everyday living and meeting the permanent citizens can one feel the fullness and rich beauty that is offered. The passive beauty of Pass Christian is no secret to its residents -- from the geniality of its people emanates a spiritual grace filled with unshakable hope for each new day of adventure and pleasure.

Some say the Legacy of the *Pass* permeates a tranquility that no other community on the Gulf Coast can offer. Others claim the mystique of Pass Christian is imbued by its transcendental ambiance. Everyone affirms that there is an essence of feeling that is indescribably magnificent.

Laissez les bontemps roulér!
Let the good times roll!

Early Cottage Development

Although a few early settlers established dwellings at present day Pass Christian in the 1700s, most of the French landholders lived around DeLisle and Wolf River. The entire peninsular shore line of Pass Christian was a pasturage for cattle that were tended by slaves of the Widow Asmar. At her death, she left the central part of the peninsula to one of her freed slaves, Carlos.

The channel in front of the present day harbor was sounded by d'Iberville and Bienville in 1699, later named for Christian d'Ladnier, who established a cattle farm and his family on Cat Island. Early on, pirates were aware of the area. Black and white pirates, both, had sailed from the Carribean Islands and south Louisiana to visit the area for lengthy intervals and some remained to homestead.

Prior to the Battle of New Orleans, in 1811, Captain Flood represented the American government by planting the American Flag and appointed Philippe Saucier of DeLisle as justice of the peace to govern the area. Dr. Flood reported that the population along the Coast was sparse, consisting of a few black families in residence at the Pass.

Steamboat service was inaugurated between New Orleans and Mobile in 1827, and lighthouses were constructed at the Pass and at Cat Island in 1831. Some years prior to 1831, Charles Shipman had acquired 600 feet of Gulf shore property, part of which he developed for a hotel. During the passage of several years and changes of ownership, the initial hotel compound was transformed into the majestic *Pass Christian Hotel*. It was there that plans were laid for a regional sailing regatta that was followed by the formation of the first yacht club in the South, in 1849. In the meantime, fashionable boarding houses and small select hotels were being built near the developing harbor where a Market Place had been erected in 1835.

This was the setting that John Henderson, a U.S. Senator, encountered in 1837. He and his associate group of developers began selling portioned lots to investors and prospects who were visiting the area as an escape from the heat and unsanitary conditions in the crowded cities of New Orleans and Natchez. The coastal towns of Bay St. Louis, Pass Christian, Biloxi, and Mobile were becoming famous as health resorts and vacation spas.

Each *"Watering Hole"*, or hotel spa community, pitted against the others in providing superior services, exceptional cuisine, and superlative room and suite accommodations. The maturing hotel industry began to build elegant wooden structures that provided fine accommodations with all the amenities for comfort to their guests, both in winter and summer.

The major road was along the ridge following the shoreline. Road surfacing was first covered with sawdust and later with clam shells. John Henderson built a few small summer cottages which he promoted and sold to newcomers. As more and more lots were sold, the new landholders started construction of their own.

Typical was a two-room Creole cottage with nogging construction enveloped by foot-thick double-brick exteriors which were plastered inside and out. The wall plaster was mixed with deer hair for strengthening and preserving qualities.

Dwellings were built with exposed beaded beams and beaded baseboards that are still found in the nuclear core centers of remodeled antebellum homes. Cypress blocks were used for foundations with hand-hewn planks for ceilings and cypress beam roofing rafters were covered with green shingles. Huge framing timbers were fastened together by wooden pegs and many of the homes were adorned with hand-carved woodwork.

As families began to make their length of stay longer because of Yellow Fever and other diseases at New Orleans, architects were brought in to design more elegant housing with tall columns and prominent roof lines. As lots were sold and measured off east and west of the Lighthouse, the distance reached further, eventually ranging to two miles on either side of the beaconing tower. There were local livery stables where a horse drawn carriage or tally-ho could be rented. Hackneys were also for hire at the local hotels. In time, affluent residents had there own carriages shipped over. On weekends they would make their outings with elegantly attired coachmen perched high on their seats and "the fair occupants, fan in hand, reclined back on their cushions in graceful but indolent repose."

Reflections which still remain true

Following the Civil War, excerpts from letters printed in the New Orleans Times-Democrat described the sentiments of the people who visited the "Pass" during its resurgence of activity.

"Its groves of oaks and magnolias and its surrounding forests of pine are covered with perennial verdure. Their evergreen foliage produces the impression that one is in the midst of a region of perpetual summer; and this impression is not far wrong as the climate is so mild that roses and violets bloom through the short winter."

"In the drive along the sea . . . the tourist sees a long succession of luxurious residences in park-like grounds; extensive boarding-houses with rustic benches scattered along the flower-bordered and shrubbery-shaded walks; and hundreds of pretty cottages with hammocks swinging lazily."

"The numerous fishing and promenade piers, pagoda-ornamented and projecting into the Sound are used for fishing or moonlight flirting, according to the bait used. The waters are more frequented by Spanish mackerel, the famous pompano, the shoal loving flounder . . . frequently speared by pleasure parties."

"The shapely hulls of vessels lying at anchorage . . . show that boating and yachting are among the liberally patronized amusements here."

"Sailing excursions out to the islands and around through the Bay are the most popular amusements. One of the favorite excursion points is a great shell mound on the banks of the Wolf River."

"Immediately in front of Pass Christian is one of the largest oyster beds in this portion of the Gulf. A fleet of 40 or 50 is busy collecting these inexhaustible stores of seafood." "The sea-shooting on the nearest islands is fine, ducks, geese, curlew and snipe being found in abundance. Quail shooting is fair. Splendid deer and turkey shooting is enjoyed by camping parties."

"It could be hardly otherwise here, where the soil may laugh up its harvests of luscious fruits and delicious vegetables to the tickling of the hoe, and the sea gives up its miraculous Galilean profusion of fishes."

"In summer it is a scene of perfect rest, languorous, delicious siesta-inviting rest; lulled by the tuneful rhythm of ripples breaking on the sandy beach and sweetened by the soft sea breeze that comes stealing over the soothed senses, fresh and pregnant, as if it were breathed form the amorous mouth of Aphrodite."

"In winter it is a picture of blue skies and green groves, bending and waving the south wind."

1920 Pass Aerial Photo

Manifesting its Heritage

Pass Christian has a wealth of History and an impassioned citizenry reaching deep into its past. It is rich in folklore, legend, myth and tradition. Unfortunately, much of its documented history has been lost. Early municipal, school, and church documents have lost their contiguous chain due to fires or hurricanes. Hurricane Camille recently took its wrath on educational and religious records. The earliest City Hall minutes book dates to 1877, even then, with missing years after that.

Therefore, it is through the efforts of the Pass Christian Historical Society, the Musee' Bourdin, record collections at St. Paul's and Trinity and other churches, and the many residents who realize the need to seek out their attics and closets to help preserve and recreate. The cement enclosed steel vault at the Pass Christian Historical Society provides a protective security for documents. At a minimum, it is suggested that copies of originals should be preserved.

Early research writers who have made significant contributions and have supplemented Pass Christian's historical record loss, are: John Lang, Nap Cassibry, J.J. Hayden, Ronnie Caire, and William Wiegand.

Pass Christian Historical Society

The founding incorporators were Liz Prichard, William Wiegand, and George Morse; who filed the Charter with the Secretary of State on March 6, 1966 as a non-profit, non-stock civic improvement society.

The Mission of the Society is:
● To work for and towards the improvement of the City of Pass Christian, and;
● To strive for the establishment of a museum or museums in which works of art, historical documents, and other matters of historical interest pertaining to the City of Pass Christian and the surrounding area of the State of Mississippi would be maintained.

Its By-Laws further include:
● To research, collect, preserve, and display subject matter pertaining to local history, and;

● To assist in the preservation and protection of noteworthy structures of historical significance in the City of Pass Christian that lend themselves to the benefit of education, pleasure, and general welfare of its citizens and visitors.

Membership in the Pass Christian Historical Society is open to all residents for a nominal annual dues subscription which includes informative monthly meetings, a newsletter, and a gala annual Christmas cocktail party. Headquarters are located in the building that was built for the Bank of Pass Christian, in 1910. The original bank vault stores many archival records and heritage artifacts.

One of its annual events in tribute to the Pass's heritage is its annual *Tour of Homes*. This fund-raising event is supported by residents throughout the community who open their homes to visitors.

Billy Bourdin Historical Collection

In the recesses of Bourdin Bros. Plumbing Shop is an organized accumulation of archival records, newspapers, and memorabilia from times gone by. The walls of the front room of the shop are fully covered with pictures and photographs detailing much of Pass Christian's history from the late 1800's and early 1900's. Pictures from before and after Camille and a display cabinet filled with artifacts and remnants from local diggings.

A visitor can get the full benefit of a museum curator, as Billy Bourdin entails the historic revelations of each of the hundreds of hanging photographs. But, more than that, Billy will tell you a few tales and yarns which would cause a lemon to smile. He started his collection many years ago which has resulted in many people bringing in their documents and pictures to add to the resources vital to the compilation of Pass historical data. With almost total destruction by Hurricane Camille, most of the "Pass's" public buildings including St. Paul's

Church and Trinity Episcopal Church, resulted in much of the original archives and official documents being lost.

Because of the expansive newspaper collection that Billy has preserved, through protracted research on his part, he has sifted out and sorted specific subject information. He has diligently made xerox copies assembled into more than 300 files (and growing) of subject category information which provides a quick reference for locals and visitors seeking out specific sources. He stands ready to help anyone or any organization in their research and discovery from the resources he has available.

In the past, Billy has also kept himself busy on the Pass Christian Planning Commission and the Historical Society. His fellow members, are always in need of access to past historical references.

Billy always cautions anyone in the Pass, the Point or anyone along the Coast, to turn in their hoarded documents which are decaying and becoming unreadable as they remain stored in attics. Much of these documents are usually left behind for someone else to toss out with the garbage pickup. He urges everyone to bring in their photographs and newspapers or even scrapbooks for his scrutiny or safe keeping.

As a result of his efforts, there has developed a genuine interest by residents to pass by the *Musee' Bourdin* (Bourdin Brothers Plumbing) to drop off a photo or some archival relic. This increased community support re-energizes Billy's efforts to continue building these significant archives. ***Unfortunately, Billy has passed.***

The Historic Preservation Commission

Pass Christian Ordinance #496 created an Historic Preservation Commission which provides the procedure to establish Historic Preservation Districts and to designate archaeological, historical, cultural, and architectural landmarks and landmark sites.

The Commission serves as a "Review Body" to review proposed work in Historic Preservation Districts and on historic landmarks.

The Commission provides the criteria for evaluating a proposed activity and standards and procedures to prevent demolition of buildings or structures by neglect.

The Commission was established to preserve, promote, and develop the historical resources of the City having as its main purpose, the protection, enhancement, and perpetuation of cultural, architectural, archaeological or historical properties of merit

Preservation commissions are authorized under revised state statutes dating to the late 1970s and early 1980s' in Section 39, Chapter 13.

Mississippi Department of Archives and History

The Director of the Mississippi Department of Archives and History also serves as the State Historic Preservation Officer. The staffing is divided into various divisions, one of which is the Historic Preservation Division. Besides monitoring nominations to the National Register of Historic Places, it oversees the Mississippi Landmark Program.

To qualify for registration in the National Register of Historic Places, is a procedure worth doing even if time consuming if the structure meets the guidelines. The Mississippi Department of Archives and History provides a Preliminary Questionnaire for anyone interested in submitting their property for nomination.

A basic requirement for the structure candidacy is that it be a minimum of 50 years since its original construction. Exterior and interior photographs must be enclosed with the questionnaire response before the state will undergo a preliminary assessment. There are still other steps which may change from time to time, before a qualified nomination is ultimately registered.

Once a structure is registered, it must comply with all regulations since a registration designation is one of the highest forms of recognition bestowed on properties by the state of Mississippi and offers the fullest protection against changes that might alter a property's historic character.

The Department has a program to oversee those Preservation Commissions which are "Certified." Periodically, the Preservation Division may also make a resurvey of existing Historic Districts .

Pass Christian Historic District

Following the extensive devastation by Hurricane Camille to Pass Christian beachfront properties, concern arose in the citizenry for the further loss by demolition to existing historic structures. There was no preservation commission or protective ordinance in place, therefore three resilient residents, Pat Mowry, Betty Rogers, and Otis Trepagnier contacted then state senator, Nap Cassibry, to assist them with the necessary requirements for creating an Historic District.

After determined research, Nap Cassibry advised the group on the proper procedure and the necessary paper-work processing that was needed for submission to State and National Archival agencies. Former State Senator Nap Cassibry offered to meet with the group and a city alderman once they decided on their course of action.

A meeting took place in Pat Mowry's home that was attended by former Alderman Charles Logan, Betty Rogers, and Otis Trepagnier, where Nap Cassibry informed them and instructed Logan on the required City Resolution that had to be adopted by the City Council in order to move the plan forward. This occurred in 1976 with the support of former Mayor Steve Saucier.

Once the adopted resolution was presented to the Mississippi Department of State Archives and History, the group was notified that they would require a $5000 cost outlay for the necessary architectural site surveys and the processing of nominating forms .

Pat Lowry once more called for Nap's assistance by stating, "now that we have the City resolution and the State concurrence to proceed with a survey, the problem now is the fee coverage for a $5000 survey." Nap went back into action and contacted Elbert Hilliard, Director of the Mississippi Department of Archives and History, they both appealed for the State to underwrite the cost of the survey on a pro bono basis. With considered reservation, concurrence was eventually effected, resulting in a two-year survey that required a definition of the proposed Historic District, house to house detailed architectural descriptions, and photos of each house with home ownership verification.

Finally, in 1979, the completed nomination forms were submitted to the National Register of Historic Places with the Department of the Interior.

Due to the efforts of these few interested individuals, the Pass Christian Historic District has resulted in preserving the nature of the homes and the heritage of one of the single-most in-tact heritage districts in the United States. This beautiful beach front could have been lost to uncontrolled housing developments and further destructive renovation constructions, which would have destroyed the essence of Scenic Drive and the other community residences that are a part of the defined Historic District. As a further result, all interested residents who owned or acquired property in the District, have been able to benefit by low-interest federal loans, providing that they adhered to the exacting compliance of State and National heritage rulings for the Historic District.

One of the first Federal grants issued was secured by Robert Goff in 1980. In full compliance with the new restrictions, "*The Fitzpatrick House,*" now the "Blue Rose," was fully rehabilitated and listed in the National Register of Historic Places.

These volunteer efforts initiated the Pass Christian Historic District and the placing of homes on the National Register of Public Places.

The Making of Scenic Drive

The seawall that divides the Mississippi Coast mainland and the Mississippi Sound was completed in 1926, primarily as a hurricane damage management measure in order to restrict erosion and destruction of the old roadway system that followed along the coastline ridge.

It was just ten years before, that Albert Aschaffenburg, a visionary native of New Orleans, formed the *Motor League of Louisiana* that had sponsored early road construction to the Gulf Coast.

Many of the interested participants also owned summer residences in the Pass. Aschaffenburg arranged with Governor John Parker of Louisiana, also a Pass resident, to use convict labor to build the *Honey Island Road* through the swamps to reach Pearlington. This new road cut driving time in half. Until then, driving from New Orleans to Logtown, on the Mississippi side, originally took four or five hours.

Between Pearlington and Logtown there was a cable ferry that crossed the Pearl River. The route continued to Slidell and to the Rigolettes where there was a shell road that led to Chef Menteur where there was another cable ferry to access New Orleans.

Between Bay St. Louis and Pass Christian, there was the Drackett Ferry that crossed the Bay. The ferry line continued until 1928, when the wooden automobile bridge was built.

At that time the roadway between New Orleans and Mobile was known as Route 701,

prior to it being transferred into the developing national interstate system when it was renamed Highway 90.

The old Highway 90 roadway ran through Bay St. Louis and at Upton Street crossed the wooden bridge into Henderson Point in front of where *Annie's Restaurant* is now located. It then continued approximately on its present course, except at midtown Pass Christian, Scenic Drive or Beach Avenue as it was called, was also Hwy 90.

In 1955, construction of the new divided highway system along the beachfront was begun, however, prior to its completion, citizens were up in arms waging a battle against the Mississippi State Highway Commission.

They argued to maintain the current Scenic Drive as part of the two lane westward traffic flow. The State won the battle and constructed the two-lane highway ribbons as they exist today.

In the end, the East Beach Boulevard residents won by losing, because now, Scenic Drive is an exclusive drive with controlled speed limits that courses along the tree-lined residential beach haven.

Pass Christian Garden Club

The Pass Christian Garden Club was first organized in 1930, and was reorganized in 1950. The local club maintains a full calendar of informative meetings and showcases an annual *Pilgrimage of Homes* in conjunction with the Regional Garden Clubs. The club historians have maintained annual scrapbooks which has valuable information pertaining to those homes which have been shown during the Pilgrimages and the flower gardens and trees of the area. The Wildflower Garden on Menge Avenue is in perpetual care by members of the Garden Club, as well as their annual ceremonies in planting a tree in capitulating their successes in maintaining the Pass as a certified "Tree City - USA."

Majestic Oaks of the Pass

On each Arbor Day, the Pass Christian Garden Club performs an observance by way of a Planting ceremony, or as in 1990 and '91, a Tree Tour. Such ventures sustain the city in being certified as a *Tree City USA*. To receive this national acknowledgment, a city must meet four standards: a Tree Board, a Tree ordinance, a comprehensive community Forestry Program and an Arbor Day Observance. Ms. Shirley Doe was very active with the Garden Club and the Tree Board in rewriting City Ordinances, the Tree Commission's by-laws, and the promotion of the 1991 *Tour of Trees*. Coral Trepagnier was also quite involved in leading a group to measure trees over 100 years old. They were able to register more than 100 such majestic oaks in the Pass excluding the older trees which were already registered.

The Pass Christian Tree Ordinance was originally passed in 1979. It regulates the removal, cutting, or damaging of Live Oak and Magnolia trees. The Ordinance controls such trees measuring a minimum of 18 inches in diameter or having a circumference of 57 inches at the height of 36 inches above ground. Non-compliance penalties are $500, or 30 days in jail, or both. Each time a tree is removed in the Pass, it must be replaced with the same type of tree.

Shirley Doe explained that Live Oaks grow rather fast when they are young but growth is slow in later years. In determining the age of Live Oaks, bore samplings do not always render accuracy. Therefore, a tree must be measured for its circumference at four to four-and-a-half-feet above ground level. That circumference measurement applied to a formula renders its age.

The largest Pass Christian Live Oak tree was located behind the house now located at 516 E. Second Street at Lang Avenue. Unfortunately, it died of old age around 1930. It was known as the *King of Oaks* in the South, even larger than the great *Friendship Tree* in Long Beach.

The Majestic Giants listed below have all been registered. The 13 trees in War Memorial Park are named, but the plan to place tree plaques at each Live Oak has never materialized, therefore no one knows which one is George, or Abraham, or Andrew, or ?

Registered Live Oak Trees in Pass Christian

Name	Location	Name	Location
Legier/Keller Oak	710 St. Louis	William H Harrison	E. 2nd off Menge
Ross B. Guest Oak	710 St. Louis	Bielenberg Oak	305 E. Scenic
Le Grande Chene	621 St. Louis	Mexican Gulf Group	305 E. Scenic
Parker/Butler Oak	St. Louis at Cemetery	Livingston Oak	533 E. Scenic
Council Oaks (2)	Pass High - West 2nd	Mullaly Group	541 E. Beach
Harry Peneguy	234 W. 2nd	Donlin-Anderson	601 E. Beach
Miramar Oak	242 W. 2nd	McArthur/Frye Grp	613 E. Beach
James Oak	248 W. 2nd	Donna Oak	701 E. Beach
David's Group	252 W. 2nd	Salatich 1 & 2	801 E. Scenic
Northrop Group	275 W. 2nd	Billups Oak	957 E. Scenic
Lang Oak	Scenic and Hiern	Bell Magnolia	1580 E. 2nd
Courtenay Oaks	110 W Scenic	Two Oaks	11 Wisteria
Slowe Oak	111 Beach Drive	Donlin-Anderson	Donlin and E. Beach
Jill Joe Oak	111 Beach Drive	Cook Oak	4119 Menge
Mc Bride Oak	240 W. Beach	Mary Patricia Group	4442 Menge
Les Chene des Keel	218 E. 2nd	Byrne Family Group	4525 Menge
Spence Oak	252 E. 2nd	Dedeaux Group	Hampton/DeLisle
Roland Martin Oak	410 E. 2nd	Windy Hill Oak	25258 Notre Dame
Gentle Oak	420 E. 2nd		
Shelter Oak	543 E. 2nd		
Morris Group (7)	619 E. 2nd		
Ascletius Group(7)	619 E. 2nd		
Catherine Young	625 E. 2nd		
Glenn Leigh Oak	625 E. 2nd		
Rosebank-Doe Oak	642 E. 2nd		
Onward Soldier	E. 2nd and Hackett		

War Memorial Park Group

George Washington, Thomas Jefferson, Abraham Lincoln, Zachary Taylor, John Adams, James Monroe, James Madison, Andrew Jackson, Martin Van Buren, Benjamin Franklin, Jefferson Davis, Booker T. Washington, and Betsy Ross.

Castles in the Sand

With the building of the New Orleans, Mobile and Chattanooga Railroad in 1869, later acquired by the L&N Railroad Company, Pass Christian became a winter resort for northerners seeking to escape the cold. Beach front hotels and boarding houses spruced up to cater to the visitors. These were imposing wooden structures providing fine accommodations and all the amenities for the comfort of their guests, both winter and summer.

But calamities struck these quarters – not hurricanes, but fire.

The famous Pass Christian Hotel burned in 1877, and later replaced by the Magnolia Hotel which burned down in 1915. The Lynne Castle also burned down in 1915. The Mexican Gulf Hotel burned down in 1917. Others were razed and put to other uses, while the only remaining hotel, the Crescent, is now a Bed and Breakfast.

The most active Historical site in Pass Christian

The current Miramar Lodge Health Care Center at 216 W Scenic Drive is the historic site of one of the most magnificent Resort Hotels ever designed.

The beginnings of the **Pass Christian Hotel** transpired in 1831, ultimately bringing to Pass Christian and the entire Gulf Coast "such a grandiose facility that all later hotels along the Coast mimicked it." Local historian and educator, Charles Sullivan is credited with stating, "Antebellum Pass Christian was not a town that possessed a hotel but rather, a hotel that possessed a town." The opening of the Pass Christian Hotel put the village on the map. The hotel had promoted itself as the *"best watering-hole on the Lake"*, denoting that the Mississippi Sound was an extension of Lake Pontchartrain. Sullivan continued, "Most of our citizens who have a keen scent for good living, like sociability, love a good bottle of wine, and relish a joke, make the Pass Christian Hotel their favorite stomping ground."

There were several false starts and changes of operators during its first years on the property that was owned by Charles Shipman, who originally purchased the lots from Edward Livingston. Shipman was one of the early post War of 1812 visionaries in forecasting the Pass's destiny.

In 1838, the *New Orleans Daily Picayune* announced that a wharf, *the "Steamboat Wharf,"* had been constructed large enough to transport horse carriages from mooring ships. The West Wing of the hotel had also been completed.

By 1839, the Hotel added new growth to its complex. The main living quarters originally housed 50 families. Large editions included a main dining room, a ballroom, a billiard room, a bowling alley, and, stables and bathing houses.

With ongoing renovations, it had a main dining room, a ballroom, billiard room, bowling alley, stables, and bathing houses. The hotel began to take shape, it consisted of a center section with a wing on each end with a wide front gallery.

It became the main stopping place because it was located only a short distance from the boat landing. To the rear was built a "Texas", so named for its use as a bachelor's guest house similar to those provided in Texas which accommodated hard-drinking, male desperados who stayed up all night gambling and being rowdy.

In 1848, a reception and grand-ball was given in honor of General Zachary Taylor, the Mexican War hero who was elected President two months later. On the following day, thousands attended a barbecue in his honor, as the General sat at a table placed atop an Indian mound in the live oak grove near the hotel.

Although officially known as the Pass Christian Hotel, it took the name of "Montgomery's," for its affable manager R.H. Montgomery who was regarded as the Prince of Inn Keepers.

In 1849, hotel manager Montgomery announced the first Racing Regatta on the Coast. It brought to life the Southern Regatta Club. This was the second oldest Yacht Club in the Country with New York being its first. Following its founding, it was eventually moved to New Orleans and renamed the Southern Yacht Club.

Montgomery was a grand promoter. Every weekend, entertainment was scheduled with grand balls, afternoon teas, and local and imported dance bands. For many years, it was the main stopping place. Commencing with 1853, the hotel remained open all year long with summer guests from New Orleans and Winter guests from Northern states. With the Pass Christian Hotel as its focal point, cottages were being built extending out, East and West, along the shoreline. For this reason, historians report that Pass Christian wasn't a town with a Hotel, but a Hotel which possessed a Town.

The Hotel closed in 1861 with the onset of the Civil War. Following the War, in 1865, the Hotel was purchased by the Christian Brothers under the auspices of St Mary's College. Brother Isaiah was expedited to supervise a crew of workmen to remodel and renovate the huge structure. It was opened as a foremost Catholic Boy's College known as *Pass Christian College* enrolling its students from all over the World in competition with Princeton College.

Brother Isaiah also originated the first College Band in the United States. It was composed of a 24-member Cornet Brass Group which started a universal trend. However, with the scourge of Yellow Fever in 1867, ten of the Brothers died resulting in hampering the school's success. Its Pastor, Father Georget, spent his life's savings attempting to keep the school open, however it finally closed in 1875.

The College was purchased and the buildings were remodeled to reopen as the Pass Christian Hotel once more. No other hotel surpassed it until it burned down in 1877.

In 1886, the razed site was purchased by Reverend Dr. H.C. Mayer who constructed several buildings for an elite girl school. The Trinity School for Girls was called the *Pass Christian Institute.* However, this school was destined for failure.

On December 1, 1894, a new group of hoteliers, A.G. Proctor and E.C. Davis remodeled the campus buildings constituting 40 apartments centered on ten acres and named the *New Magnolia Hotel*.

In 1901, a 9-hole Golf Course was laid out promising to be the finest on the Gulf.

Following a second remodeling, it was renamed the *Magnolia Hotel* which, unfortunately, burned down on April 1, 1915 due to a fire in its attic.

The McGlatherys bought the site and built the *Miramar Hotel* in 1916. Sam L. McGlathery, son of J.M. McGlathery, worked with the Hotel as well as Editor of the Coast Beacon newspaper (the predecessor to the Tarpon Beacon). McGlathery was also the first President of the Chamber of Commerce in 1923.

In 1937, it was operated by Walter Read and was purchased in 1952, by Mr. and Mrs. Douglas Black. In 1957, it was temporarily called the *Old South Motor Lodge*, until 1959, when the Douglas Black investment group converted the Hotel into the *Miramar Nursing Hotel* and hired poet-laureate of Mississippi, Earl Cuevas as its Administrator. That building was razed in April 1964 to build a new nursing home facility.

The new nursing complex opened on July 1, 1966 with the renovated 100 bed nursing and convalescent home called the *Miramar Nursing Village*. The facility consisted of two buildings with 50 beds each joined by patios on the 5-acre site. In 1974, the LMM Management Corporation of Baton Rouge acquired the business and the property with some renovations. In 1976, a new 72 Bed Wing was added bringing the total to 180 beds. In the 1980s, Bill Reed, now of Long Beach, leased the buildings and acquired the business. As of 1994, the current owners are the Delta Health Group of Pensacola. With the growth and demand of the nursing facility, it has a waiting list for tenancy.

Lynne Castle

The Lynne Castle was formerly the Rev. Dr. Savage's old Episcopal School that was located on Beach Road. It was purchased and renovated by Louisiana Supreme Court Justice Lynne B. Watkins, and elegantly furnished for his private home. Finding it too large, he converted the estate into a 23 guest chamber house in 1892 and placed it under professional management, continuing to call it the Lynne Castle. The large guest chambers accommodated mostly weekly or season guests, and did not cater to transient trade. It occupied the square from U.S. 90 to St. Louis, and from Clarence Avenue to Henderson Avenue where the former 3-story Richelieu Apartment building and where the Jitney Super Market and shopping complex is now located.

In Charles Dyer's *Along the Gulf*, in 1895, he stated, "in arriving at Lynne Castle and being particularly impressed by the beauties of the building and its situation, we alighted and passing through the gate, sauntered leisurely up the long walk to the house, where we were hospitably received and were shown over the place. Lynne Castle is something of a family resort, being a house of twenty-three large guest chambers capable of accommodating about sixty people. From the genial proprietor we learned that the house was started in 1892, since which time it has had a phenomenally successful run of patronage, both during the summer and winter, for Lynne Castle like several other of the hotels at the Pass remains open all the year round.

"The house is situated in the center of spacious well shaded grounds and form the front a beautiful lawn stretches down for fully one hundred yards to the front street. It makes a beautiful play ground for the children and is especially adapted for croquet, lawn tennis and other out-door games, while at the side under the shade of stately trees, hammocks and swings may be put up for the guests. In front of the grounds a long wharf extends out into the Gulf with a large bathing pavilion at is end in which will be found all the usual conveniences. For those however, who are not in very good health are do not care to stand the cold plunge in the waters of the Gulf, there are hot and cold water bath rooms specially constructed in the house, which, by the way is supplied with artesian water, which from its analysis, is known to be of great medical value."

"As for the table, it is unsurpassed, it being supplied direct from the city markets, while unlimited supplies of fish, crabs, and oysters can be drawn from the Gulf. From the wide verandas of the house a beautiful view of the Gulf may be seen dotted here and there with the white sails of pleasure crafts, and those whose taste incline towards sailing, sea bathing or fishing, they have an excellent opportunity to indulge in these pleasures. Lynne Castle is the summer home and the property of Hon. Lynne B. Watkins one of the judges of the Supreme Court of Louisiana who finding too large for his family leased to the present management. Judge Watkins nevertheless spends his vacations at this beautiful resort. Lynne Castle is beyond a doubt the most exclusive hotel on the entire coast. Taken altogether this house is an ideal family resort, both in the winter and in summer, and those who can secure accommodations there consider themselves quite lucky."

Soon after the Judge's death, Mrs Watkins sold the property to I.T. Rhea, who continued to operate the hotel as the Lynne Castle

The building was lost to fire in 1915. Two weeks later, the Magnolia Hotel took flame.

A Grand Winter Hotel on Davis Avenue

The Mexican Gulf Hotel Company of Pass Christian was organized in 1882 by Gen. George Sherman and other stock holders with an authorized capital of $35,000. Before the building was half finished it was found that the cost would be far in excess of the subscribed capital stock. The whole plant cost was about $105,000. Doors were opened to guests on June 16th, 1883, with M. J. Crawford as manager.

With the opening of the Gulf Ship Island Railroad between Chicago and Gulfport being completed, it was the first hotel on the Gulf Coast that was specifically designed to

attract winter guests from northern states. The hotel was constructed in the Colonial style of architecture with covered verandas and observatories overlooking the Gulf of Mexico. The three story structure faced Davis Avenue with 250 guest rooms equipped with hot and cold water, telephones and all modern conveniences including private baths which were arranged singly and *en suite*. The building was steam heated throughout and had an elevator providing access to the upper floors. It was designed without inside rooms resulting in every room sharing direct sunshine.

A private pier extended out from the hotel property into the Gulf. It was a spacious-covered structure, providing seats where guests of the hotel could enjoy breathing in the salt air while surrounded by boats of all kinds.

Through its beginning years, the outstanding indebtedness began to cause trouble. The company defaulted on the bond interest and they were brought to court and eventually foreclosed upon. The Stockholders led by Frank Howard leased the hotel to hotel manager Crawford who also struggled along until he spent all of his money and was finally forced out by his creditors in 1887.

Matthew J. Crawford, a fine writer of his memoirs, reported the following account. "Some twenty years or so ago a gentleman of means living in Pass Christian on the Gulf Coast of Mississippi conceived the idea of building a hotel at that charming spot. To this end he engaged the cooperation of some bankers and cotton merchants of New Orleans in the undertaking. This gentleman was a very pleasant person, and like many pleasant people knew very little about hotel construction and the manner in which it should be conducted when built.

He was obstinate in his views and as those who were associated with him knew even less than he did about such matters he was allowed his own way in everything. In consequence, when the hotel was completed, instead of facing the Gulf, it offered by a small front, two rooms deep overlooking the water. As the house was designed for a summer and winter resort, and as everyone stopping at the hotel wants a front room, the house, when opened, was unable to supply the demand, there being only four front rooms having a view of the Gulf. My reputation having preceded me, such as it was, I was selected to manage it. I left New York for the *Sunny South* and upon my arrival took charge of the hostelry. I had many acquaintances and friends in New Orleans, so I felt that I would like to be among them. The house opened early one summer and by July we were fairly under way. The clientele was entirely Southern. Sugar and cotton planters from Louisiana and Mississippi and New Orleans and Mobile families attended by an army of colored servants. The children and servants made up nearly half the house count, and invariably as the summer season came 'round also would appear the whooping cough and then it was a sight to see the "fussed up" manager vainly trying to quarantine the afflicted babies so as to prevent the mothers of the well ones not to depart and leave a lot of vacant rooms on his hands."

"We would hardly recover from this plaque when we were dismayed by the yellow fever scare. When the first rumors of their fever broke out everybody scampered to their homes to escape being quarantined. It was no joking matter to be left inside the lines. Every little hamlet established what they were pleased to call a *"gunshot quarantine"*, and if one approached the lines with the intention to cross them, he was promptly ordered to return, or else he would be shot *"full of holes."* There never was any yellow fever at the "Pass", but there might as well have been for the real thing could not have been so thrilling as the scare. I struggled through six years and was then forced against my will by the sheriff to return to New York. My exit was hastened by this official having had a judgement placed in his hands

against me, and some of my friends having told me of this man's ways of collecting bad debts, I kissed my hand to Pass Christian and left it to its fate."

A former administrative employee of the hotel, Bernard Chotard, then leased the hotel, which was later followed when S.F. Heaslip took over the hotel in 1894. Samuel Heaslip had served several terms as mayor of Pass Christian and is remembered for reorganizing and spearheading the formation of the current Pass Christian Yacht Club, in which, he became its first Commodore in 1893.

Heaslip renovated the hotel extensively and provided lighting and heating to the 250 guest rooms and chambers. The beautiful dining room was one of its greatest features, which was lighted on three sides by long French windows that reached from the floor almost to the ceiling. During meal times, the tables were crowded with guests as the Black waiters went about silently supplying the many wants.

Charles Dyer, author of *Along the Gulf*, stated in 1895, that, "The Mexican Gulf Hotel is by long odds, the finest hotel architecturally on the entire coast, and its interior decorations and furnishings are beautiful in the extreme."

"No pains were spared to obtain all the delicacies of the seasons. There are two enormous fireplaces here on which logs placed on chilly evenings throw out a grateful warmth and light, which, reflected on the bright colored carpets and hangings, make the place look cheery and homelike." More than all others it is the favorite resort for Chicago, St. Louis, Cincinnati and other northern and western people, who during the winter months come to the Pass in large numbers."

One of these winter vacationers in 1913, was President Woodrow Wilson who dined at the Hotel restaurant while staying at the Dixie White House.

Albert Aschaffenburg was the last hotelier to invest in the hotel. He brought together a group of investors from New Orleans. They bought and remodeled the *Mexican Gulf Hotel* in 1916, only for it to burn down on January 8, 1917.

At that time, there still was no firefighting equipment in Pass Christian. The Gulfport fire engine was called and reached the scene in about 40 minutes, but due to low water pressure, it was unable to perform. An engine from Biloxi also responded to the call, but before its arrival the walls of the massive building fell. A large number of firemen from Bay St. Louis walked across the three-mile railroad trestle since there was no automobile bridge at that time. Meanwhile, from Long Beach, Gulfport, Biloxi, Delisle, and Cuevas, large numbers of people were attracted by the flames that lit up the heavens. Needless to say, in the following year firefighting equipment was added to the volunteer *"Bucket Brigade"*.

The Grey Castle

This was the site of an elegant Victorian home in the 900 block of East Beach Boulevard (Scenic Drive) and Menge Avenue which was owned New Orleans ship chandler, J.H. Menge. Menge let John L. Sullivan use the facilities to train for the Sullivan-Ryan fight that took place on February 2, 1882, on the grounds of the old Barnes Hotel in Mississippi City. It became the Grey Castle Hotel in 1929 when its owner Edward Buckner of Jackson made the transformation. At the time, there were no operating hotels when his secretary persuaded him to convert his home by adding wings to each side that were built by contractor Frank Wittmann in December 1929. The nucleus was a rambling Queen Anne house with all bedrooms having an outside view, each with private baths and showers. The Grey Castle Hotel was promoted as a family hotel and was the last hostelry built in Pass Christian. The

project included not only the hotel on the beach but a colony of cottages built around many oak and pine trees and beautiful lawns managed by Mrs. William Coutourier. The Grey Castle Hotel thrived during the early 1930's but soon folded due to the Great Depression. Ralph Hicks bought the Hotel in October 1941 and operated it for 8 years. It had 49 rooms with large closets and individual tiled bathrooms. In 1950, the structure was purchased by the Jesuit Catholic Order for a Seminary at which time, the name was changed to Xavier Hall. It was later used as a Catholic Retreat for vacationing and retiring priests. In 1957, the Jesuit's of New Orleans occupied part of the large edifice as a temporary home for the Provincial Superior and his staff. After the Jesuits moved out, Xavier Hall, as it was called, continued as a Retreat Home and the Oblates from Pine Hills moved in following the Camille damage to their Bay area facility at DeLisle.

As a result of the Brothers in training at Pine Hills and the Jesuits and Fathers in "retreat" at Xavier Hall, the Catholic churches throughout the area were benefitted by many members of the Clergy, many of whom performed Mass in meeting their holy obligations.

Xavier Hall was eventually sold and torn down which resulted in two new residences built at 915 and 919 Scenic Drive.

Inn by the Sea

The Inn-by-the-Sea was a dream come true. It was situated in the center of a beautifully landscaped 75-acre park, with a private white-silver sand beach extending from the very edge of the patio to the emerald waters of the Gulf of Mexico, with no roadway to cross. The Inn-by-the-Sea resembled a Spanish castle, as if lifted bodily from old Spain and gently set on the romantic Gulf Coast of Mississippi.

One could almost expect to see Spanish Grandees or French Cavaliers strolling through the rough-hewn beams of its corridors. One could almost imagine waking in the morning to witness a duel beneath one of the majestic Live Oaks. The very atmosphere of the Inn was

charged with romantic intrigue of the *Spanish Main* and yet it had all the creature comforts in catering to the slightest wish of a vacationing family.

The former owners of the Inn, Mr. and Mrs. I. T. Rhea, who 1915, had lost to flame the "Lynne Castle Hotel", once reflected on the beauty of just sitting on the beach in front of the *Inn by the Sea,* and watching the magnificent sunset. They encouraged their guests to join them in listening to the splash of the waves and to become alert to the many natural amenities that were waiting to be reaped. They maintained flocks of exotic birds. In the patio, they hand-fed the bugle birds adorned with gold and black plumage, along with the white cockatoos,  parrots, and beautiful macaws. The Innkeepers organized picnics into the piney woods and alerted their lodgers to absorb the glorious sunshine and to feel and taste the tang of salt air.

Everyone learned to forget their cares as they would take a venture by sailing on the *Pussy Cat* or the *Queen of the Fleet,* or in taking a cruise on the *Oneida* to the barrier islands where they would spend the afternoon plunging from the bow into the Gulf's emerald waters.

The **Inn-by-the-Sea** was a delightful hotel surrounded by cottages between the tall pines and moss hung live oaks basking beside the shores of the Gulf at Henderson's Point.

This was during the early '20s before the Bay bridge was built in 1928. The Dracket ferry was still operating between the town of Bay St. Louis and the Point. Like the many other old hotels of the Pass, the Depression of the '30s reaped its toll. At the beginning of World War II, the Inn was taken over by the Merchant Marines as a training academy only to be abandoned at War's end.

That same area now facilitates the $13,000,000 Gulfshore Baptist Assembly. Since its groundbreaking ceremonies in 1972, Baptists from every state and territory, visit the educational and religious retreat. In addition to a large auditorium and conference facility, extensive dormitories house hundreds of students with separate living quarters for counselors.

Pine Hills

During the mid to late 1920s, the Pine Hills Hotel and Golf Club was situated on a fine tract of land on the north shore of the Bay of St. Louis, between the mouths of the Jourdan River and the Wolf River. The place was formerly called "Shelly" from a large mound of clam shells that supposedly had been accumulated by Indians during times past. Present day access can be made by way of the Kiln-DeLisle Road next to the Dupont Plant south of Interstate Ten.

A group of Louisianians and Mississippians took interest in the Pine Hills Resort Hotel as a sportsmen's rendezvous. The clubhouse itself, on the Bay of St. Louis, was an architectural gem, containing 186 rooms, arrangeable in suites for family groups. The hotel cost more than a million dollars to build with furnishings that were considered the height of luxury and beauty. It was in the center of an estate of more than 2000 acres and even more acreage was under lease for duck shooting. It was hard to find better quail in the South than in the open lands of southern Mississippi. Other game was found there too, doves, turkey, squirrel, etc. The Pine Hills Club had secured rights to even more thousands of acres of available land in their planning to establish a great game preserve.

On the club grounds, kennels were maintained where 60 of the best hunting dogs in the South had been housed under the eye of skilled trainers.

The Club was also rather keen on horseback riding. Its stables contained a number of select mounts that followed beautiful bridle paths throughout that part of the piney hills Coast.

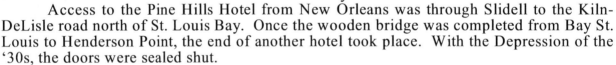

The 18-hole golf course was recognized as one of the most interesting and one of the most sporty on the Gulf coast. The Golf Club House was constructed with great logs, and catered to many professionals as well as amateurs.

Boating was promoted all year long and fishermen from the area touted 589 different varieties of fish to be found in the Bay waters.

Access to the Pine Hills Hotel from New Orleans was through Slidell to the Kiln-DeLisle road north of St. Louis Bay. Once the wooden bridge was completed from Bay St. Louis to Henderson Point, the end of another hotel took place. With the Depression of the '30s, the doors were sealed shut.

With the need for coastal defenses and training, the hotel was taken over by the U.S. Army during the early to mid-1940s.

Laying dormant and vacant for a number of years, the old Pine Hills Hotel seemed like an ideal location for the Oblates of Mary Immaculate Religious Order to establish a major Seminary. Even though the priests and brothers were all from the Mid-west, they purchased the hotel and grounds in 1953 and officially opened Our Lady of Snows Scholasticate (popularly known as the Pine Hills Seminary).

The first clergymen arrived in mid-year to take on the mammoth job of cleaning and conversion of the hotel to a seminary. The first ordinations of priests took place in 1955 and they finally closed down in 1968.

It was during the Summer of '73 that the Dupont site planning team decided to effect feasibility studies in the area of Pass Christian to establish a plant facility which would produce titanium dioxide.

Land options were made in the Bay area, five miles north of Pass Christian between the old Pine Hills Hotel and the DeLisle community. The plant was initially expected to be constructed over a 30 month period and to be completed in 1977.

In January 1984, Du Pont finalized a purchase of the 25-acre Pine Hills Hotel property in addition to the surrounding area bringing an 80-acre increase to the original 2200-acre complex. It has been primarily utilized as a "Good Neighbor" buffer zone and the Du Pont Employees Recreation Area.

<table>
<tr><td>1920's Aerial Photo of the Pass</td></tr>
</table>

This is a photograph of Davis Avenue during the early 1900s' showing the Mexican Gulf Hotel on the right with its wrought iron fencing, some of which is still utilized today. On the left near front is the Northrop Building and immediately north of it is the old Hancock Bank building as it was and still remains today as an office building. Further down, was the building where the first Bourdin and Martin businesses started operating in 1932, which later, burned down. The Mexican Gulf Hotel at right, burned down in 1917.

Lost Forever

Not just Hurricane Camille, but also losses due to other calamities such as fire or willful demolition has resulted in decimating many of the original old homes of Pass Christian. The West End as it was once called has lost many houses. Just driving westward on West Beach Boulevard leaves a sense of virgin lands which have remained undeveloped. Prior to Hurricane Camille there were only three Highway 90 vacant lots ranging from Henderson Avenue to the curve at Henderson Point.

Along that route were many of the oldest homes that fronted this shoreline because not only John Henderson, but Edward Livingston before him, had sold lots to such early builders as Mrs. Plum, who may have built the first house in the area, and there was the Knox house, and the Calvert house, as well as others.. John Henderson built his private residence at several places because he would sell each one to any willing buyer. When he built houses he also built roads to get to them. On occasions he would buy them back at a higher price than he sold them for, only to turn around and sell them at a greater profit.

Some of the lost houses include those that the Henderson's have been credited for constructing. Since the original great loss to Camille, a number of new homes have replaced the many that were lost. In some cases small subdivisions now stand where plantation style mansions once existed. In many cases, complimenting vintage structures have been rebuilt, while others have restored their homes in architectural styles in conformance with past heritage in the Pass.

Lost Homes or buildings along West Scenic Drive/West Beach Boulevard/Hwy 90

100 - Old City Hall at Market, 101 - Old Chamber of Commerce, 103 - J.C. Ellis, 104 - Roy's, 109 - DeMetz, 111 - Liversedge, 114 - Phelps, 200 - Old School now New City Hall, 236 - Reynoir, 238 - Peneguy, 242 - McBride, 244 - Hillyer, 248 - Hammett, 252 - Tucker, 414 - The Richelieu, 418 - Griffith, 420 - Terrell, 500 - Keenan, 508 - Peat, 512 - Schmidt, 524 - Smith, 608 - McCollough, 616 - Smits, 624 - Balch, 628 - Sharp, 702 - Sharp, 730 - The Dorothy Dix, 738 - The Simpsons, 740 - DeVries, 748 - Bagg. 752 - Fairley, 754 - Witherspoon, 760 - Oustalet, 784 - Ellis, 786 - Wahl, 794 - The Breakers, 808 - Chauvin, 812 - Amos, 816 - Stauffer, 820 - Marquez, 822 - Holcomb, 830 - The Simpsons, 834 - Jahncke, 902 - Gildersleeve, 908 - Lindstaeder, 910 - Landry, 916 - Salavant, 918 - Brenza, 922 - Robin, 1004 - Jung.

Lost Homes or buildings along East Scenic Drive/East Beach Boulevard/East Hwy 90

102 - Crow's Nest, 108 - Griffon's, 110 - Jerry's, 112 - , 114 - , 116 - Namis, 123 - Fixit Shop, 125 - Adams1, 126 - Adams2, 128 - St. Paul Rectory, 154 - Kozy Shop, 202 - Rick, 204 - Spence, 210 - , 214 - Allen, 222 - Yelverson, 231 - Hayden, 238 - Hanson, 254 - Bufkin, 258 - LaRosa, 424 - Claiborne, 767 - Dixie White House, 915 - Grey Castle, 1101 - Richardson, 1219 - Rafferty, 1225 - Phelan, 1305 - Malty, 1307 - Randal, 1313 - Lobrano, 1317 - Ewing, 1321 - Gulf Air, 1345 - White, 1411 - Kittiwake, Gulf Palms, 1506 - Murphy Oil, Moonlite Drive Inn, 1586 - Catalina Motel.

Vanished Mansions
Ghosts along the Coast
Lost Forever – the Dixie White House

The old home, when owned by the Herndons was called *Beaulieu*. It was said to resemble the inclusions of both the Cabildo in New Orleans and one of the wings of the original White House in Washington. The mansion was artfully crafted with stately columns and arches that dated to the 1850s.

During the early 1960s, the "Dixie White House" owners, Mr. and Mrs. Claude Schneider, were considering the demolition of the historic old home. Members of the Pass Christian Garden Club were dismayed by the threat of its destruction. In solution to their problem, they recruited newcomer Liz Pritchard, who arm in arm with Ruth Gordon, then secretary of the Pass Christian Chamber of Commerce, formed a committee to preserve the old mansion. This action was the impetus that lead to the formation of the Pass Christian Historical Society with several fund-raising promotions that followed. Even the Schneiders became members and temporarily staved their plans to tear down the building.

However, as time passed, the drive for funds floundered, and in 1966, as matters seemed bleak, their prayers were answered. Mrs. Thomas Jordan, on visiting the vacant home, decided she wanted the place as a summer residence. On October 5, 1966, in celebration of the act of sale, Mrs. Jordan was formerly welcomed at a meeting of the Pass Christian Garden Club which was joined by members of the Pass Christian Historical Society.

One of the grand home's earliest owners was retired General William S. Harney, a famed cavalryman of the Mexican War and the Indian Wars. In 1880, he hosted former President U.S. Grant.

In the winter of 1912-13, President Woodrow Wilson celebrated his 56th birthday with Miss Alice Herndon as hostess. She was the daughter of the former owner, Mrs. Thomas Herndon. At the time of President Wilson's visit, the home was actually owned by Mrs. J.M. Ayers of New Jersey, in which state, Wilson, in 1910, had been elected Governor after having been president of Princeton University. Later, a member of the Ayers family sold this home to New Orleans engineer, A.M. Lockett.

The house was described as a roomy home that was a fine example of Colonial architecture, modified by the old French and Spanish tiles which prevailed in Pass Christian in earlier years. The structure was set on massive arch columns of old Spanish architectural beauty. There was a fireplace in each of the six bedrooms with high ceilings and wide windows. The dining room table was habitually set for 25 persons. One of the bathtubs was imported Italian marble weighing several tons.

Historically, the home was built in 1854 by John Bache of New Orleans. He sold it prior to the Civil War to George Jones, president of the Canal Bank of New Orleans. The next owner was General William Selby Harney who saw action in the Florida Indian campaigns and won fame in the Mexican War for bravery and leadership. He received additional fame in the campaigns against the Sioux Indians in the northwest. Although in active service during the Civil War, he was retired in 1863, because of suspicions that he was a Southern sympathizer. The Dixie White House was razed following heavy damages due to Hurricane Camille in 1969.

Lost Forever – Ossian Hall

Ossian Hall, a former palatial mansion was once located at East Beach. It was built by Louisiana sugar and cotton planter George Seth Guion in 1848. George Guion married Catherine Lucretia Winder with whom three children were born, Lewis, Walter, and Carrie (who married former Louisiana Governor Gen. Francis T. Nicholls).

The home was originally called the old Miltenberger Place and the name was changed by 1939 owner, J.F. Galloway to Ossian Hall.

The house became famous in 1919, with the filming of the silent movie, *Come Out of the Kitchen,* starring Marguerite Clark. She was no relation to a later owner, C.C. Clark, who had a daughter named Margaret.

Beautifully structured, the large white two-story Greek Revival had a wide double-deck portico fronted by four immense fluted columns. The 14-room mansion had a colorful history that included such guests as Andrew Jackson and Benjamin Butler. Listed among the last owners were: C.C. Clark, followed by James Galloway, and then Col. Hulbert DeBen, owner at the time it burned down in mid-July 1956.

Lost Forever – Henderson Mansion

According to J.J. Hayden's research, in the 1830s a large house was situated in the center of the tract of land now known as Henderson's Point. There is some evidence that John Henderson may have occupied this home in 1839.

Located in the 700 block, this home was known as the J.B. Simmons Mansion during the 1920s to 1950s, because he had increased the height of the original structure and added the tall white columns which fronted it. In 1956, Dumas Milner bought it for $75,000.00.

In 1968, it was scheduled to become Coast Episcopal private high school and to open for the September 1969 session. Instead, it was demolished by Hurricane Camille.

Prior to Simmons, the property was owned by Robert Norman of New Orleans and William J. Montgomery, who had married Sadie Parker, sister of John M. Parker.

William Wiegand reported that the adjoining Moring property was formerly the home of Dorothy Dix, which burned down in the 1950s and was purchased by Dumas Milner.

Tour of Pass Christian Historic District
Scenic Drive and Beach Avenue
Non-conforming homes are excluded, while driving from East to West

All of the two-and-a-half miles of Scenic Drive are within Pass Christian's Historic District which includes 330 acres and consists of 119 dwellings and buildings. City preservation ordinances throughout the years have changed during intervals of new governing officials, but for the most part, most of the homes have abided by national historic preservation restrictions.

During the antebellum period, most construction produced mainly summerhouses, which were single-story structures with a gable roof and usually with three or five bay windows with an inset gallery. Styling was often a blend of Greek Revival, Queen Anne, and local vernacular ranging in size from cottages to mansions. Through the construction periods evolving from the 1830s, 17 varying architectural styles have been defined within the Historic District.

Many of the stately mansions and cottages were built by wealthy New Orleanians when the Mississippi Coast was considered their playground. The original cottages were constructed of brick walls that were more than a foot thick covered with wall plaster mixed with deer hair for strengthening and preserving qualities. The huge framing timbers were fastened together by wooden pegs and the homes were adorned with hand-carved woodwork, tall columns, and prominent roof lines.

Houses erected after 1865 were usually larger and often featured hipped or gambrel roofs with inset dormers.

As years passed, Pass Christian residents showed an increased tendency to hire architects to design or to re-design their homes. Colonial Revival architecture became popular in endeavoring to be homogenous with the older structures.

In 1979, the Mississippi Department of Archives and History wrote the following plaudits on the architectural qualities of Pass Christian.

> *Despite recent building losses due to a devastating hurricane, Scenic Drive remains the largest architecturally intact major 19th Century resort area in the South and one of only a few in the nation like Cape May, New Jersey, and Newport, Rhode Island, both of which are National Historic Landmarks that have managed to retain most of their original character.*

Nearly all of the homes in the Historic District have specific historical architectural characteristics for which they are registered in the National Register of Historic Places.

These homes are regulated by the Pass Christian Historic Preservation Commission and monitored by the Mississippi Department of Archives and History.

Many of the mansions also have preserved or restored the outbuildings which usually consisted of a garconniere, or servant quarters. Originally these were used as bachelor quarters or guest houses.

Also predominant were gazebos and *"Shoo-flies."* A shoo-fly was usually built around a large Live Oak for its shade and the platform was raised from the ground ten-feet or more in order to optimize the breezes of the beach in addition to sit above mosquito habitation levels. These platforms were decorated with a lattice facade and usually painted white.

Although some homes are small and may seem insignificant by comparison to the mansions which are also located in the Historic District, they are treated with equal significance to the preservation of Historic value. Since new owners may apply for permits to change a building's structure, they may ultimately cause remodeling/destruction which is prohibited by the State as well as the Preservation Commission. The ruling guidelines protect all genuine historic structures from obliteration from their original architectural design. Nevertheless, on occasion, complications arise with attempts to modernize historic buildings while still attempting to preserve their historic features. Resolution can usually be accorded by following careful and expert examination in accommodating both preservation and modernization.

As an example, vernacular Greek Revival cottages were indigenous to the Mississippi Gulf Coast area both before and after the Civil War. A typical galleried French colonial cottage was characterized by its "T-shaped" floor plan with a gallery that swept around the arms of the "T" to entirely encircle the main body of the building. Settlers on the Gulf Coast developed this method of construction in order to maximize the capturing of breezes and to provide ample porch space for escaping the sun's direct heat during different times of the day. The fact that this is the very same basic design array for Jefferson Davis' *Beauvoir*, illustrates that it was practical for use in mansions as well as smaller cottages and bungalows. Although once quite numerous, a large percentage of these houses predominated along the Gulf Coast. However, much of the architectural heritage has been destroyed or remodeled beyond recognition making the ones remaining both rare and significant. It is for this reason that Pass Christian's Scenic Drive is unique.

Pass Christian is also home to many of the Majestic Giant Live Oaks along the Coast. Many of these oaks, including magnolias, have been registered with their appointed age classification along with their names. A number of these trees can be closely observed while driving slowly along tree-lined Scenic Drive and Second Street. Specific Majestic Oaks aged greater than 300 years are denoted by an * following the street address with the homes as listed herein.

In this panoramic review, the residence street address is listed first, then the date or approximate date of its construction; followed by the generally accepted historic name of the property, if any.

Much of the Architectural descriptions that follow were derived principally from the 1979 nomination forms drafted by the Mississippi State Archives Department for the National Register of Historic Places. Most of the photographs were taken in 1989 by Billy Bourdin and were selected from the Bourdin Historical Collection.

A few home locations have had more thorough site heritage research performed, therefore more information being reported herein. In most instances, current owner names have been omitted, unless their names had been prominently made known in news articles relating to their homes.

A few Architects and Builders of Note

One of the earliest architects was James Gallier, who built and designed Gallier Hall, the old City Hall in New Orleans – he also built and designed the home at 753 E. Scenic. More recent New Orleans architects were with the firm of Koch and Wilson who performed modifications to 525 E., 533 E., 651 E., and 1024 W. Scenic.

An early businessman was Clausel Courtenay who built his own homes at 313 E., 507 E., and 651 E. Scenic. The Wittmann family had a number of *"Frank"s* as their first name, unless the builder was recorded as Frank Wittmann, Sr., the others were a son, or cousins, or nephews. The Wittmanns, as builders, modified or renovated 413 E., 419 E., 427 E., 513 E., 519 E., 549 E., 607 E., 613 E., 625 E., 641 E., 829 E., and 961 E. Scenic. Jim Wittmann built the house at 118 ½ W. Scenic Drive.

A more recent builder contractor was Horace Labat who worked on a number of homes, one of the last ones being that at 733 E. Scenic.

The McDonald family had a progeny of masons who performed work on many of the houses and outbuildings in Pass Christian.

The Grand Tour in this book proceeds from East to West to allow motorists to easily view the homes as they procede along Scenic Drive's beautiful umbrella of live oaks that offer shelter and shade.

The Pass Christian Historic District encompasses many beautiful homes.

For purposes of touring these homes, the listing commences from the East starting in the 900 block allowing drivers to have access to the street lane closest to the homes.

Touring drivers should drive slowly and hug the curbing when stopping in order to allow traffic to pass by safely.

Many homes have a property marker as

displayed in this photo. Nearly all of the homes along Scenic Drive have complied with registration requirements with the National Register of Historic Places.

961   1890
Baldwin House.
"Villa Karma" is a handsomely detailed two-story frame Queen Anne Cottage home which was remodeled in 1937, by Frank Wittmann. It has an exterior brick chimney on the east side which features stone quoins. It is noted as being stylistically significant enclosed by its cast-iron fence. A prior owner, George Maginnis, contracted with Frank Wittmann to remodel the house..

Historic Note: Sometimes known as the "Haunted House", it was the setting for a mystery novel, *"Cobweb House."* Legend has it that an original owner in the 1890s, killed his neighbor during a drunken spree. Since then, other mishaps have continued to occur, such as smoke being reported in the home when there was no fire.

Historic Note: Confederate troops were garrisoned at this site during the War between the States. Some prior owners were William Dufour, George Maginnis, James Burk, George Moring, Charles Klump.

947　1900

Extremely well-proportioned one-story, frame, five-bay Colonial Revival cottage with a graceful bell-cast hip roof. Inset gallery with fluted Doric columns. Gracious turn-of-the-century variation on the popular coast cottage form. Numerous rear ells. The residence is set back providing a brick walkway to the front gallery. Six bed-rooms and four baths with a tennis court, swimming pool and cabana to the rear. Some prior

owners Or tenants were Pete, Picone, Andy Lee, O.V. Thomas, E.H. Fairchild, Bewettt McElhiney, Wm Montgomery, Col. David Sandlin, O.S. Montagnet.

943　1849

Classic coastal cottage with center hall, two-room-deep design. Complete one-story, frame, gable-roofed, five-bay coastal cottage. The inset gallery has square columns. Double-leaf doors with glazed upper panels service the gallery. There is a late 19th century addition to the eastern elevation. Marvin Mingledorff had the home remodeled in the 1970s. *Historic Note:* This home was built by Roger Hiern, a sea captain turned real estate agent. He sold much of the

early lands as an agent for Edward Livingston and later for himself. He built the Lighthouse at the site of present City Hall and was its first Light keeper. His brother was Finley B. Hiern, first Mayor of the Pass in 1838. After the 1969 coastal wrath of Hurricane Camille, the house was restored by the Mingledorff family the following year. A white picket fence fronts the property. A prior owner was Louise Waring, and another was Marion Mitchell. Other owners or tenants included C.L. Chapotel, Mona Royster, Gertrude Warren, J.K. Bolton, Fernand Demourell, Bernard Schotty, Alfred Penn, Maurice Stockton, Marvin Mingledorff, Byron Simson, C.N. Monstead, T.S. Monstead.

939   1905

The two-story frame, gable-roofed dwelling has broad overhanging eaves that are set with Japanese brackets. A large gabled balcony defines the central entrance bay. A porte-cochere is fixed to the eastern elevation.

This house became one of the early tests between the owner and the City's Preservation Commission, which restricted some architectural changes that were requested. The

owners eventually challenged the Commission by claiming they would give the house to a religious cult such as the Hara Krishnas or a Muslim group. Needless to say, the requested changes were not adopted. In response, a spokesman for the Preservationists declared that ugliness, like beauty, is in the eye of the beholder. Such contests as this has resulted in educating potential buyers on alteration restrictions pertaining to historic homes or structures within the Historic District. A wrought-iron fence fronts the property. A prior owner was George Hoffsett.

927   Undated - Not Listed

This two story, Colonial Revival home has a protruding portico which is embraced by four rounded columns across its front, with a fan window above the main door entrance. A porte-cochere is attached to the West wing with a dormer. The extended East wing also includes a dormer. The residence is boldly shuttered and

distinguished by a Widow's walk atop the roofline.

Historic Note. This was the site of the Eslick House, originally built in 1890 for S.F. Heaslip who was Mayor of the *Pass* in 1886 and the first Commodore of the Pass Christian Yacht Club. The former Eslick House caught fire and was later torn down. A prior owner was E. Martin

923   1920

Soria-Soule Home. The monumental, eclectic two-story, stuccoed dwelling has a tiled hip roof and is bracketed by overhanging eaves. The central entrance bay is defined by a flat-roofed semi-circular Tuscan-columned portico. The cobblestone driveway and impressive iron fence was added with elegant drive-way entrances. The house was enlarged by W.C. Soria and was remodeled by Leon Saloum. *Special Note:* Previous owners of the Soria home

were the Henry Ware family, then, later, by the Soule's of the New Orleans Soule Business College. Later, it was occupied by A.J. Kern for the Kern School for Boys, during the 50s and 60s. Other owners included C.A. Callums, Leon Salloum, Marlin Torgeson, and Kent Nicaud.

919   Undated
Not Listed.
Clement Home.
This Coastal colonial style home was designed by architect Barry Fox and built in 1986, as a two-story frame with front gallery adorned with thick round columns. Chimneys protrude from each side of the large hip roof from east and west extensions. Bay windows adorn the second story.
Historic Note: This was the eastern portion site of an elegant Victorian home

which became the Grey Castle Hotel in 1929, when its owner, Buckner, made the transformation. Ralph Hicks bought the Hotel in October 1941, and operated it for 8 years. In 1950, the structure was purchased by the Jesuit Catholic Order for a Seminary and the name was changed to Xavier Hall. It was later used as a Catholic Retreat. However, due to heavy damages from Hurricane Camille, the Jesuits razed the building and sold the property to J.E. Monroe, which resulted in two new residences being built at 919 and 915.

915   Undated Not-Listed Toulmin Brown Home. One story colonial cottage with round columns across the front gallery of the main section with east and west wings. This 1978 home has an impressive portico centering the structure with a fanned window above the doorway. A porte-cochere is attached.

Historic Note: This site was the western portion of the

Grey Castle Hotel, and later, the Catholic Retreat known as "Xavier Hall." A former owner of the property was Frank Mendoza.

905   1900   This richly detailed one story and a half, frame dwelling is distinguished by its set gable-end to the street. It is a raised, enlarged one-story, five-bay coastal cottage. An octagonal-ended addition on its eastern elevation features a Tudor Revival chimney. The inset gallery with square columns wraps around two sides. It is adorned with denticulated cornices.

Historic Note: This house was built by Charles Francois DeMetz who arrived from Nancy, France to Pass Christian, in 1852. The two homes at 901 and 905, were built after his marriage, He had sent home for his inheritance which arrived in the form of gold pieces. Some of the prior owners or tenants were Col. H.P. Rinsgdorf, Thomas Heitzenberg, D.W. Blake, Lt.Gen. Doyle Hickey, Gen. H.K. Mooney, and Joel Blass.

901   1915

The home is a one-story frame hip-roofed bungalow with distinctive asymmetrical massing. A hip-roofed eastern wing was added with extensive remodeling. A rear service ell connects the house by a hyphen structure. Prior owners were Blake and A.A. Grant.

Historic Note: This home site was one of two adjoining houses built by Charles Francois DeMetz after he arrived in Pass Christian, in 1852. He courted and married the widow Josephine Patenotte

Martin who was the great, grandmother of Roland Martin, former owner of Martin's Hardware on Davis Avenue.

MENGE AVENUE

Named for Capt. J.H. Menge, a New Orleans ship chandler, the northern reaches of this street was first known as the Pineville Road. At its northerly course it merged with Red Creek Road and became one of the major roads for farmers bringing their produce to the Coast after the closing of the original road that crossed from Cuevas to the VFW Hall, originally, then known as the *Trade Palace..*

861   1849

The McCutchon-Butler House.

This beautiful one-story, five-bay, Greek Revival dwelling has a classically inspired flat-roofed gallery, which is supported by simple square columns carrying a stylized entablature. After being built by the Bethea family, Samuel McCutchon acquired it in 1853.

Historic Note: After the Civil War, Lt. Col. Sam and Adelle McCuchon left for Belize to escape Federal troop oppression, while members of the family continued to stay at the home.

Historic Note: It later became the dwelling of Col. Edward George

Washington Butler and his wife Frances during the 1870s. Frances Butler was the great-granddaughter of Martha Washington and grand niece of George Washington. It is reported that she planted the still blooming Camellia bush which she had carried from the Mount Vernon estate. An imported japonica that is more than a century old, still thrives here. Both Butlers are interred in Live Oak Cemetery where historic markers were placed by the Daughters of the American Revolution. A prior owner, oil painter Mrs. Allen Rendall.

855   1920
This frame hip-roofed vernacular dwelling has a two-story central mass which is flanked by one-story wings with inset galleries. In the rear of the property is a detailed story-and-a-half servants quarters. A white picket fence fronts the property.

Former owners of this home were Elmer Northrop, Sherod Willett,

Elmer Northrop was a prominent businessman, operating Northrop's General Store at the corner of Davis and Beach Boulevard which also housed the Hancock Bank's first coastal branch.

During the 1850s, there were more than 100 piers extended from Pass Christian shores out into the Mississippi Sound. Today, only ten piers have survived the peril's of storms and neglect along Pass Christian's water frontage and just a few are actually functioning as originally intended.

849   1849

Formerly the *Harrison-Balter House.* Before and After photos are portrayed on this page in elucidating an excellent example of historic preservation by restoration. The original structure was a one-story frame, nine-bay, hip-roofed, vernacular, Greek Revival dwelling with an inset gallery fronted by octagonal columns. Some earlier modifications had been made, however, significant renovations and rear-end additions were performed by Dr. and Mrs. Harry Danielson. The home is now called the *Belle B'Anne.* Despite major damages caused by Hurricane Camille, Dr. Harry Danielson and his wife elected not to demolish the original

homestead following their purchase. in 1990. Instead, they restored the complete complex including the main building as well as the out-buildings.

Restoration and preservation efforts lasted 18 months. The process included shoring the house with jacks and balancing it upon railroad ties. Dirt fill was poured in to provide an adequate foundation. The original roof slates were removed individually, cleaned, and replaced one by one. All original doors, frames, door-knobs, hinges, etc. were painstakingly removed, refreshed, and reinstalled. The restored house consists of 10,000 square feet of space, containing six bedrooms and five and one-half baths. When purchased, the house measured 5,000 square feet, but with new found uses for the attic and cellar, this vastly increased the square footage without effectively changing its original appearance. The stately 128 foot front gallery, with its authentic iron railings, is supported by 16 original columns. A wrought-iron fence fronts the property. *Historic Note:* The earliest structure at this site was built by Jilson Harrison in 1848. That house was replaced in 1849 with the customary four-room Coast cottage. This structure remains today as the front of the existing home, altered in 1893 and 1905 with further additions. Some prior owners were Col. Bluford Baltar, Santos Oteri, and John Kolp.

845   1964

Contributory Rating:

Monroe House.

This large, two-and-a-half-story, mottled brick, hip-roofed Colonial Revival house was built on the site formerly occupied by two earlier houses. Stylistically compatible with neighboring structures, the Georgian style home is located on an 800 front foot trace comprising of 8 acres of land. It was built by J. Edgar Monroe of New Orleans.

Historic Note: One of the houses torn down was the

Hart-Harrison one-story, frame house at 831 E. Scenic Dr. The other house was listed as "845" and known as the *Villa Rosehart* by the Sullivan Family. Prior owners to the original house at this property were Jacob U. Payne, Charles Coffin, Charles Ziegler, William De Pass, Swan Sullivan, the Portas Family and the Luria Family.

Special Note: This residence is the largest house per-square-feet in the State of Mississippi. 1997 additions by Chuck Ramsey family expanded it to 30,000 square feet. Its wide and spacious grounds spread out along Second Street to its rear with elaborate landscaping and abundant trees. A tall wrought-iron fence fronts the property.

829   1850

McCutchon-Ewing House.

This handsome hip-roofed, frame, Greek Revival dwelling was raised to two stories in 1938 by John Ewing. A stilted-arch arcade supports the impressive flat-roofed portico which is set with square columns. The elaborate Federalesque frontispieces date from remodeling performed by builder Frank Wittmann, Sr., in 1939. Wrought Iron gates predominate the front driveway entrances.

Historic Note: Percival McCutchon called it *Carlisle Place* for his wife, Rebecca Butler's hometown in

Pennsylvania. Some prior owners were Dave McCutchon, Fred McCutchon, Eugene Aschaffenburg, John Ewing, Henry Clay, R.E. deMontluzin, the Brig. Gen. L.F. Loesch family, Percy Monroe.

811   1885

This picturesque raised story-and-a-half, frame, gable-on-hip-roofed cottage is characterized by an inset gallery with Tuscan columns and turned balustrade. It has full-length four-over-six windows facing the gallery. The pedimented dormers have a sunburst motif in tympanum. It is noted as being one of the most distinctive late 19th century cottages in the Historic District. It is fronted by a white picket fence.

Historic Note: This house was built by Ernest W. Dreiholz similar to his home in Ramos, Louisiana. The 22-foot living room has a glass enclosed sun porch behind it. Some prior owners were Captain Drackett who owned the ferry line crossing between Bay St. Louis and Henderson Point, Mr. and Mrs. Leon H. Ferrier, Robert Morris, Reggie Gable, Martin Macdiarmid, Dr. George McHardy, Karen Graham who was the Estee Lauder girl, S.L. Drum, Nauman Scott. The house was also used by A.J. Kern as a dormitory for the Kern Academy.

805   1900

This large, asymmetrically massed, two-story, frame, hip-roofed, Colonial Revival cottage is significant with its double-tiered gallery and Tuscan columns. The central cross gable with palladian-motif fenestration gives the illusion of symmetrical massing. Full-length windows service the gallery. The home was extensively remodeled by the Bernadas family in 1986.

Previous owners included E.D. and Marcelle Cambon, A.D. LeJeune, Percy Sandal, William Haynie, Henry Kinney. Extensive remodeling was performed in 1986, by its current owner.

801*   1920
This quaint home is a long, low, one-story frame bungalow-vernacular cottage. The shed-roofed gallery shelters its facade. The shed-roofed dormer distinguishes the structure populated with a range of four small casement windows. Numerous ells extend from the house.

Some previous owners or tenants were Ben Henniger, Preston Breckenridge, George Shields, Anne Duncan, A.A. Castenado Dr. Blaise Salatich.   ***Live Oak site names are: Salatich 1 & 2.**

LANG AVENUE
Named for John H. Lang, a former councilman and mayor of the City and author of his published memoirs. He was a significant businessman dealing in real estate, livery stables, funeral parlors, insurance and participated in the early business development at Gulfport.

Historic Note: At the east side corner of Lang Avenue was located the *Dixie White House* which was demolished due to heavy Hurricane Camille damages. It was so named for the 1913 health restoring visit by President Woodrow Wilson to the Pass, as well as visits by several other U.S. presidents. Woodrow Wilson and family were guests of Miss Alice Herndon. <u>*Historic Marker states:*</u> Built by John Backe of New Orleans in 1851.

105 Lang Avenue
Late 19th Century
This homesite was originally part of the Dixie White House complex. After Hurricane Camille, the property was subdivided.
The sole remaining structure is a generously proportioned, three-bay, shingle style carriage house. The house is paneled with circular-head doors in place. The
quaint white cottage in photo is the primary living quarters and set back from Scenic Drive beside the carriage house.

765

Contributory Rating:
This two-story, brick, five-bay, Colonial Revival dwelling was built in 1972. It has a Tuscan-columned porte-cochere on its east end.

Prior owners were Lee Spence, William Geddes

Historic Note: The house was built on the west portion of the former Dixie White House site, which had been severely damaged during Hurricane Camille in 1969.

757   1890

Davis Cottage. This raised, one-story, frame, hip-roofed cottage has an inset gallery. The architectural structure was detailed to complement the styling of an earlier cottage next door at 753. A white picket fence fronts the property.

Some prior owners or tenants were Irene Davis, D.C. Griffith, Adm. J.K. Vardaman, Fredrick Fritz Swigart, Paul Montjoy, R.C. Bittenbender, Garci Moran, Conrad Kuebel, Dr. Kent Andrews, Wes Jones, Dr. Susannah Smith.

Historic Note: Large kettles were found exposed in the front area

after Hurricane Camille washed over the area. These were determined to be tar kettles used in ship building and repairs.

753   1850

Seaton-Davis House.
This distinctive one-story, hip-roofed vernacular dwelling has a carpenter Gothic styling on the inset gallery. It has a paneled dado affixed both in the gallery and the central hall. An arched affect between the columns and the pitched roof creates an

interesting variation on the basic design. An early rear

cottage and carriage house still survive. It is a distinctive antebellum structure. Seaton sold his home to W. Davis. Some prior owners were Miss Hortense Davis, Stanley LeMarie,
Historic Note: Robert Seaton and his associate, James Gallier, built and designed Gallier Hall, the old City Hall in New Orleans. An Historic Marker is planted at this location. There were 3 Davis sisters, one of whom, Irene, started the Town Library.

743   1920

This home is a long, low, one-story, five-bay, frame, gable-roofed cottage with an inset gallery. It has double-leaf doors with glazed upper panels at the service gallery. A distinctive feature is the pelican statuary on its chimney stack.
Historic Note: This site was the home of William B. McCutchon. Widow Mary McCutchon sold to Wm. James and Caroline Pattison.
        Some prior owners or tenants were Andre Dedicos,

B.W. Griffith, Dr. W.K. Gauthier, Irene Weston, Dr. W.K. Atchison, Thomas Wagner, Hans Jonassen, J.O. Kelly, Joseph Landry, Bob Wright, Carl Neuenraus.

741   1926
This set-back, long, one-story, frame cottage was converted from the gardener's cottage when the main house burned in 1925. It has a facade screened by a long columned arbor supporting a mature wisteria vine. The simple structure is enhanced by careful landscaping.

Some prior owners were John O'Kelly, J.F. Kerrigan, Marguerite Craven Wilburn, Stanford Morse, Richard Hadden.

Historic Note: The Presbyterian Parsonage was built on the beach side.

737   1870s
The two-story, frame, single-pile, vernacular cottage is distinguished by a double-tiered inset gallery under a gable roof. The home originally had chimneys on east and north elevations. This two-story cottage form is unusual, and is sometimes described as slave-quarters being part of the out-buildings of a complex of structures.

Some prior owners or tenants included A.V. Davis, Allen Hackett, J.J. Hayden, Sherman Pardue.

733   1920
Hackett-Hayden House.
Also known as *"Our Anchor."*

A modest, one-story, frame, four-bay cottage with steeply pitched gabled roof. It has an inset gallery with square columns. The home has overhanging eaves, with a late-nineteenth-century cast-iron fence that encloses the property on its south boundary. The tin roof and floor-to-ceiling windows make it a classic design. Restoration was performed by Bill Kidd and contractor Horace Labat. The interior was gutted and remodeled.
Some prior owners or tenants were J.J. Hayden, Alfred Stern, James McCutchon, Eugene Hayden.

HACKETT LANE

Like most of the streets that are perpendicular to Beach Boulevard, those land holders that had cut a roadway on their boundaries to reach the back road had eventually donated or sold the right-of-way to the City in exchange for continued maintenance. This Lane was donated by Allen Hackett, which divided his property. His home was on the west side of the lane.

729   1841
Yandle-Hackett House.
This home is a one-story-and-a-half brick, five-bay Greek Revival dwelling. It has a broad, three-bay, pedimented portico set against an inset gallery. It has distinctive lintels with foliated end and center blocks with an attached rear service ell. Casement dormers were an added feature. It is one of two brick antebellum dwellings in the district. The home was built by the Yandle family of Natchez. Conveniently, there was already a brick yard on this site when purchased in 1841. Walls in portions of

this home are over a foot thick and covered with plaster. Before the Civil War it was owned by Alfred Vidal Davis. He and his neighbor cultivated grapes for the manufacture of wine. After passing into the hands of the Allen Hackett's, a strip of land on the east was donated for a north-south roadway that bears his name. This home is unusual for the Coast because it has both a basement and an attic. A white picket fence fronts the property.
Historic Note: Scratched on the outside plaster is the date, *"1839."* The base of the hallway doors are wider than the top and are called "Key" doors. One of the prior owners referred to the home as being known as the *"Old Slave Quarters"* because there was a row of iron rings fastened to the timbers supposedly where slaves were held chained. Prior owners, Mrs. Jas. L. Ewing, W.R. Berkenroad.

715   1905
This elegant home is an eclectic, story-and-a-half brick dwelling with a distinctive clipped-gabled roof form. Dominating the facade are three squat, hip-roofed, bungaloid dormers. It has a Tuscan-columned inset gallery that bows at the central entrance bay, and wraps around three sides of house. It incorporates an earlier house that was evidently similar to that at 729 East Scenic Drive. It has numerous

rear ells and attached outbuildings. A beautifully, ornate, wrought-iron fence surrounds the property. Some prior owners or tenants were Alabaman William T. Hardie, J. Thornwell Witherspoon and H.L. Swift, R.H. Hoffsett, Dr. George Byrne, Dr. V.L. Stanfield, Bin Ly formerly of the Blue Rose.

709   1840   *Legendre House.* This nicely proportioned story-and-a-half frame dwelling has an inset gallery with square columns that carry a stylized entablature. It is adorned with a cast-iron balustrade. False jibs under nine-over-nine windows on facade. It was restored in 1947 by Curtis C. Walther as a Colonial Revival style home that was typical on Louisiana plantations having a wide clapboard exterior, with tall windows, shutters and

wide galleries. The picturesque carriage house survives. A service ell with an inset gallery was moved to back of the property. A white picket fence fronts the property.
Historic Note: Edward Connery, a New Orleans ship chandler, was a prior owner who brought electricity into the house, making it the first home to have lighting in Pass Christian. He had one of the early artesian wells in the Pass. Prior owner: Dr. G.N. Smith.

701* 1845

Set-back, diminutive, one-story, three-bay, frame cottage with inset gallery. Double-leaf doors with glazed upper panels service gallery. Originally built as a Garconniere for the main house next door at 709. Extensively enlarged on the rear and remodeled by the A. M. Dantzlers. The western-most bay of the gallery is enclosed. This home was written up in *Along the Gulf* by Charles Dyer in 1895, while describing former owner C.A. Pardue's summer residence. Prior owners were: U.S. and Sarah Dudley, Ashbel Green,

Edward and Mary Green, Eliza Janvier, J.P. Egleston, Ed Richardson and Augustus May, Selby Harney, Edward Connery, Charles Pardue, A.M. Dantzler.

Historic Note: Alonzo Mayers Dantzler was an early timber businessman controlling 110,000 acres of South Mississippi forest lands. His father owned the L.M. Dantzler Lumber Company in 1888, one of the first large lumber mills.

**   * Donna Oak, 490 years old.**

COURTENAY AVENUE

Courtenay Avenue was named for the Courtenay Family

651 1875

This broad, story-and-a-half, five-bay, vernacular cottage has a square-columned inset gallery with a range of three small double-hung windows in each gable end. It has a number of rear ells. The pilastered pedimented dormers were added at a later date. It was built by Clausel Courtenay and renovated in 1974 by Koch and Wilson of New Orleans. The home has a distinctive elevator and glass enclosed gallery.

Some prior owners or tenants were Col. Levi Brown, Robert Adams, Stanford Morse, Harris Helen Carrigan, E.A. Lang.

Historic Note: The properties of 651 and 647 were where the Green Military Academy was located. One of the first automobiles in Pass Christian was owned by Miss Maud Payne. She and her sister, Henrietta, drove the yellow, low-slung runabout with its windshield attached to the steering wheel post along the shelled Beach Boulevard daily during the summer months.

647   1874

A Courtenay House.
This nicely proportioned house is a conservative story-and-a-half frame, five-bay, vernacular dwelling with an inset gallery supported by square columns with plain balustrade. It has three pedimented dormers with casement windows.
Historic Note: Before the Civil War the two houses, 647 and 651, were the site of Green's Military Academy.

Some prior owners or tenants were Clausel Courtenay, George Courtenay, Drusilla Courtenay, Courtenay Apartments, Charles Shepard, Willie Cobb, Fredrick Kohl.

641   1910

A two-story frame Colonial Revival dwelling with a double-tiered inset gallery beneath a gable roof. The gallery is set with square columns and lattice balustrade on the second level. Exterior end chimney. The home contains four bedrooms and three and a half baths. It is considered a good example of the late use of popular coastal form.
Historic Note: The home is considered as

a stylistic attribute built by Frank Wittmann, Sr. The house was designed for Mr. A. Aschaffenburg, hotelier from New Orleans, who was one of the later owners of the famed Mexican Gulf Hotel and promoter of other joint ventures in real estate in the Pass. Some prior owners were George Morse, James Winston, Miss M. McGlathery,

635   1900

This home was originally a two-story, frame, Colonial Revival dwelling with hip-on-mansard roof with an inset gallery supported by Tuscan columns which wrap around three sides. For many years, it was lived in by an ageing, eccentric multi-millionaire who allowed the cottage to greatly deteriorate. Prior to being refurbished, it had a pedimented projecting pavilion with a semi-circular portico defining the central entrance bay. John C. Ellis, Jr. purchased the home and made extensive renovations that

created its present emergence. *Historic Note:* The original home was known as *Fox Hall* as owned by C.B. Fox. In the early 1900s, the Ernest Merrick family lived here. Their private pier extended 1000 feet from the beach to the bathhouse. A youthful cousin visited one summer and because he reminded the Merrick boys of a little Lord Fauntleroy, they cast him into the Sound. After he dried off he went back to the house to practice on the piano. He continued piano drills into manhood as he became one of the world's most famous composers. His hits were: *"My Heart Belong's to Daddy," "All of You," "Begin the Beguine," "I've Got You Under My Skin," "Night and Day," "I Get a Kick Out of You," "I Love Paris," "Easy to Love," "In the Still of the Night," "So in Love," "With a Song in my Heart," "C'est Magnifique," "It's De-Lovely."*
     The young boy was **Cole Porter**.

629   1890

Wiegand House.
This is a charming Victorian, diminutive, one-story, frame, hip-roofed, shotgun-form cottage with board-and-batten rear service ell. The inset gallery shelters its original three bays. The shed-roofed side porch was added to its eastern elevation and subsequently was enclosed after 1930. A small three-bay guest cottage appears to pre-date the main house. Following many attempts in seeking approval to renovate the house, permission was given by the City by over-riding

objections of the Preservation Commission. The house was changed by replacing the roof and changing the front to accommodate six columns thereby changing the appearance from a 3-bay facade to 5-bay. *Historic Note:* William G. Wiegand, a former writer and reporter, wrote an unpublished draft of the history of Pass Christian covering many items of interest. His rough drafts/notes, photos, and mementoes were given to the Pass Christian Historical Society by his daughter, Jane Wiegand Randolph, in 1999, marking a significant archival contribution.

625   1871

Leovy-Hill House. This story-and-a-half, frame, hip-roofed dwelling with inset gallery extends to partly wrap around the eastern and western elevations. Originally, it was a single story house that was remodeled in the eclectic Colonial Revival style by builder Frank Wittmann in 1913. At the same time the second level was added with an interior curved staircase. A shed-roof dormer links to the pedimented dormers on both the south and west elevations and a

pergola-like porte-cochere is on the eastern end of the gallery. Of particular interest are the fanlights over the front door and the hip roof. *Historic Note:* Wm. H. Hardy, founder of Gulfport and Hattiesburg, owned this home after he became a Harrison County judge following his loses in building the railroad to Gulfport. He and his son were also City Attorneys during 1912-13. Many years later, his widowed wife referred to the place as the "Old Silk Plantation" because an old Frenchman had made an attempt to cultivate silk which failed due to a frost that killed the silk worms that were being cultivated on the mulberry trees. A white picket fence fronts the property. *Special Note:* Wm. Wiegand historical notes state that Henry Jefferson Leovy arrived in the Pass in the opening 1870s with his wife, Elizabeth Adair Leovy. They bought the two adjoining lots next to the Monroe family, to whom Mrs. Leovy was related. They lived here for more than 20 years.

Prior to Camille Hurricane, the home was owned by Brig.Gen. Lawrence Frederic Loesch, 1957-1965. His daughter Margaret was Executive Producer of the Muppet Babies T.V. series and more recently, in the year 2000, became President & CEO of Odyssey Network. Other prior owners included Margo Gack, Guy Billups, E. Stewart Manusell.

Still thriving, and reported to have been imported from Japan more than a century ago, is one of two of the oldest Japonica trees in the Pass.

Historic Note: In 1838, the W.G. Hewes family lived in the prior home on this site and sold it to C.D. Lancaster in 1869.. One of their sons, Finley Hewes, was mayor of Pass Christian and was appointed first mayor of Gulfport, from which position he resigned due to being called away to war.

623   1938

This set back, modest one-story, frame, cottage has a gable-ended pavilion. The main house may incorporate a portion of earlier structure that had burned some time after 1930. It has coupled fenestration with a simple shed-roofed gallery. A white picket fence fronts the property. *Historic Note:* This site and the adjoining site at 613 E. Beach, were owned by two sisters. Miss Polly (Mary Hardin Monroe) lived her life out in this one before it burned down. Miss Polly also conducted a small private school in her home with her sister, Miss Kitty (Kate Adair Monroe), who was principal of the Pass Christian Young Ladies' Institute in 1871. Miss Kitty owned the home

next door. Some prior owners were Margo Gack, Malcolm Dinwiddy, and also L.N. Grosener before the previous house burned down.

613*   1910
Legier-Frye House. This is a superbly detailed and proportioned two-story, frame, hip-roofed, Colonial Revival dwelling with some bungaloid elements. According to a prior owner, the house was a pre-fab design kit assembled by builder Frank Wittmann for John Legier, a New Orleans banker. It has a lattice-enclosed, pergola-like entrance porch and pilastered side solaria topped by roof gardens. The home is one of the most architecturally progressive and best-preserved dwellings on the beach. The low picket

fence and landscaping complement the architecture. An earlier pedimented one-story frame cottage with square-columned inset gallery remains on the property. *Historic Note:* Miss Kitty (Kate Adair Monroe) owned an earlier home on this site which was a raised basement residence that was torn down. John Legier married Henrietta Buddig of Pass Christian. They purchased this property from Miss Kitty Monroe, razed the house and replaced it with a modern house. Later the house was acquired by George H. Stanton, a Montana banker, then by Marshall Frye. ***McArthur/Frye Group, 460 years old.**

607   1882
Martin-Macdiarmid House. An early owner was Isaac Edmund Glenny who sold to Francis Martin in 1897. It is a richly detailed, raised, one-story, frame, hip-roofed dwelling. It is a late 19th century structure with an inset gallery. The house was remodeled in a flamboyant Colonial Revival style by builder Frank Wittmann.

Pilastered frontispieces with projecting cornices surround the facade fenestration. Its gallery is set with coupled, stylized, Doric columns. Pedimented dormers with decorative millwork in tympanum ventilate the attic. A white picket fence fronts the property. *Historic Note:* This property is one of the few lots which remains intact as described in the original conveyance deed. Most of the early lots fronted the Beach and extended northward to Bayou Portage or to Johnson

Bayou. This lot maintains its original depth description.

603   1905

The story-and-a-half frame dwelling has a set gable end to the street with hip-roof gallery supported by square columns. Flat-roofed porte-cochere on western end. Special Note: The house was raised from a one-story cottage after 1930. The glass enclosed porch was added with the trellis and awning facade embellishments. A white picket fence fronts the property.

In 1915, this house was one of the Chapotel rental properties.

Some prior owners were Don Eddy, Francis X. Orofino, Dr. Carroll Allen, Clark Salmon, Charles Pierson,

601*   1895

The home is an asymmetrically massed, one-story, frame, hip-roofed dwelling with an octagonal-ended projecting pavilion with a symmetrical inset gallery and battered square columns which wrap around two sides. Numerous rear additions, some apparently were former outbuildings.

Some prior owners were John Donlin, McKees, Clayton, Frank Anderson, James Drury, Mrs Martin Macdiarmid.

*Two trees – one named for Donlin and the other for Anderson, 450 years old.

DONLIN AVENUE

551   1840s
Ballymere.

A handsome, long, one-story, frame, gable-roofed, Colonial Revival dwelling having as its nucleus, an early two-room Creole cottage with nogging construction, double brick, plastered inside and out. It has an inset gallery with chamfered posts sheltering the entire eleven-bay facade. The original house core features exposed beaded beams and beaded baseboard. It is a long multi-windowed,

one room deep period piece with delicate wrought iron over the calumniates. A wrought-iron fence fronts the property.

Historic Note: Enlargements were performed in 1853 and 1928. Cypress blocks were used for the foundation, hand-hewn planks for ceilings, and cypress beams covered with green shingles for the roof. It is one of the best examples of the Colonial Revival style in the district. This cottage is a valuable period piece and is reportedly one of the oldest in the city.

Historic Marker Statement -- *Oldest existing home in Pass Christian built by Luciene LaBranche of hand-hewn cypress. Historic Note:* A frequent summer resident to the Pass was Louisiana State Supreme Court Justice Frank Adair Monroe, his sister Mary Elizabeth owned this home. Her second marriage was to Judge Joshua Baker, meeting him as he summered next door at 549 E. Beach. Their daughter, Mrs. Jules Bayle inherited the home. A prominent recent owner was Dr. Donald G. Rafferty who served two terms as Pass mayor. He donated the large West Indies anchor that is located in the front of the Pass Christian Yacht Club. Some prior owners were Donatien Augustin, Capt. John Youenes, Joseph Dubul, Francis Mouny, Antoine Dubul, Delia Herriek, George Vincent, Franklin Pugh, Dr. Donald Rafferty, JWC Wright, James Drury, Charles Klumpp, Dr. William Hopper, Kent Nicaud.

549   1850
The Cottage.

"Judge Baker Cottage" This is a typical one-story frame, five-bay cottage with an inset gallery. It incorporates the earlier three-bay house which was enlarged and remodeled in the Colonial Revival style in 1947 by builder Frank Wittmann. The gallery has since been glass enclosed. A white picket fence fronts the property.

Some prior owners were Dominic Riso, J.G. Baker, Cobb, Joseph Walker, Charles Klumpp

543   1910

This home was built by Dr. Mozart Rainold. It is a boxy, story-and-a-half, frame dwelling with both bungaloid and Colonial Revival detailing. A two-bay shed-roofed dormer projects from the gable roof. An inset gallery features truncated octagonal columns carrying a central pediment and paneled square columns. A white picket fence fronts the property.

Some prior owners were Sidney Haas who owned the Haas Seafood Factory in the Harbor that was destroyed by Hurricane Betsy in 1965, and Stanley Butte, and Gerald Yeager.

Historic Note: Earlier owner of prior homestead was Benjamin Baggett.

541*   circa 1848

This is a charming, rambling, nine-bay-long, one-story, frame dwelling with inset gallery supported by square columns set beneath a stepped hip roof. The original house consisted of the five westernmost bays. Numerous rear ells include former outbuildings now attached to the main house. Later nineteenth and twentieth century additions were made. A white picket fence fronts the property.

Historic Note: An early owner commented that, "several rooms had hand-hewn timbers and hand cut wall lathes The original kitchen, separated from the main house, had a 15-foot-long cement and iron stove. Another prior owner was Captain Henry Claus Buddig. It was reported that he had a couple of brass cannons that had flanked the front walkway. His daughter, who married Dr. Mozart William Rainold, sold the home to Colonel Roy Haggerty It was later purchased by Paul Ratliff and later, Lee Schlesinger. The current owners have extensively renovated the home in the 1990s.

Historic Note: First ownerships were Edward & Sarah York, 1842; Alexander McGibbon, 1848; Henry & Eliza Fassman, 1850; Heinemann, 1874.

*Mullaly Live Oak Group.

533*   1936
The Markle House

This is a well-proportioned, two-story, brick, hip-roofed, Colonial Revival dwelling with flanking, one-story, hip-roofed wings. It has a double-tiered inset gallery with cabinets enclosed with louvered blinds. Its fence and landscaping complements a well-preserved period piece. The fence is a combination of brick and cast iron fencing. *Special Note:* It was designed by Richard Koch of Koch & Wilson, New Orleans for Donald Markle. It was later

extensively renovated by J. Alfred Levert.   *Historic Note:* The previous home at this site burned down, it had been inhabited by Hamilton M. Wright, Augustus Reichard, the Rose Family and later descendants of the Soria Family. In the 1920s, the home was owned by the George Ferriers and by the Wyman family previously, and more recently owned by Henry Dreyfous. This was also the site of the first South Mississippi artesian well which was drilled by Alabaman John Timmons Hardie in 1884. Hardie's grandson, Francis Moore, married Lorraine Werlein of the New Orleans music publishing family. Other prior owners were Hugh Hawthorne and Alfred Nugon.   ***Livingston Oak, over 400 years old.**

525   1967
The Crosby House.

This is a well-proportioned, one-story, brick, hip-roofed, Colonial Revival dwelling based on the Louisiana plantation form. Its central five-bay mass is balanced by two-bay recessed wings. The handsome Ionic-columned frontispiece has an elliptical transom which accentuates the central entrance bay. The combination brick and cast iron fencing compliments the landscaping. *Special Note:* Designed by Richard Koch of Koch & Wilson of New Orleans. *Historic Note:* The previous house was a summer

residence of New Orleans banker Antoine Carriere who was born in Chateau Luzie, France. and later owned by Dr. Walter Schuster, Henry Dreyfus, and Jonn Vacarro, before it was torn down for the Hollis Crosby House. A set of majestic, cast-iron roosters adorn the drive-way pillars. *Historic Note:* President Taylor's son, Dick Taylor, stayed in the Pass to recuperate from wounds as received in the War between the States. While at the Pass Christian Hotel, he met and married Myrthe Bringier. Their daughter Betty Taylor, later Mrs. Walter Stauffer, spent summers during the early 1900s in the earlier home at this location.

519   1895

Breaux-Clay House. This is a gracious, two-story, frame, hip-roofed, Colonial Revival dwelling. The double-tiered inset gallery is supported by giant-order square columns. A handsome Ionic-columned frontispiece surrounds the single-leaf door with a leaded-glass upper panel and carved lower panel. A thermal windowed dormer projects from the front elevation. The two-story hip-roofed addition to the west side was built by Frank Wittmann, Sr. A porte-

cochere is at the eastern end. Constructed by Loch Breaux, it was remodeled in 1940, by then owner George Clay who named his home the *Holiday House*. Some former owners were Mrs. Caryl Broom (noted for providing drama instructions and directing community plays), Elwood Clay, Dr. Maurice Wingo, Diamond Jim Moran, Jr., Paul Westervelt. The first Toast to the Coast was hosted here. A wrought-iron fence fronts the property.

Special Note: Former owner Mrs Breaux was often quoted as saying, *"This is my home and I'll do as I damn please!"*

513   1910

Lockewood.

The picturesque, two-story, frame, chalet-type bungalow has a set gable end to the street. The double-tiered inset gallery features pergola detailing and extends into a porte-cochere on the western end. The gable end is detailed with a range of casement windows and a shallow balcony. This house was built by Frank Wittmann, Sr. The adjoining Garconniere dates from 1890. The brick and wrought iron fencing compliments the landscaping.

Some prior owners were A.G. Patterson, Joseph S. Menendez and J.E. Prichard.

511   1915

This modest, one-story, frame, hip-roofed cottage has a shed-roofed front gallery with exposed rafter ends. This chalet-style bungalow is set with its gable end to the street. The unaltered structure has a double-tiered inset gallery which features pergola detailing and extends into a porte-cochere on the western end. The gable end is detailed with a range of casement windows and a shallow balcony.

Historic Commentary:
Reportedly, this is the last

remaining original house of descendants of the former freed slave, Charlot. After being purchased by Edgar Bohn, he moved it to the south side of the street and rented it. Following the 1947 Hurricane, he moved it back to its present location north of Scenic Drive. Some prior owners or tenants were B.P. Ohr and Minor Sutter.

509   1905

Chapotel House.
This is an eclectic, boxy, two-story, frame dwelling with a double-tiered inset gallery and Mexican-style tile roof. Built on narrow lot, the driveway undercuts the second level on east side. After the house burned, it was extensively re-designed in 1926, by N.J. Karst. A wrought-iron fence fronts the property.
Historic Note: The entrance door with a circular-headed transom

was reportedly salvaged from the famed Mexican Gulf Hotel which was located at Scenic and Davis and burned down in 1917.

Some prior owners were N. J. Karst, Mrs. Morrow, Thomas Peters, A.W. Hyatt, Marvin Mingledorf.
Special Note: One of the outbuildings, a servants house, was donated by Mrs. Morrow to the Girl Scouts and moved to Fleitas Avenue and Second Street. It was destroyed by Hurricane Camille.

507   1887
Courtenay-Arnold House.

This conservative, one-story, frame, five-bay, hip-roofed cottage has an inset gallery supported by square columns. A pedimented dormer ventilates attic. It has an attached rear service ell. The home is a good representation of the popular antebellum form. It was built by Clausel Courtenay. A white picket fence fronts the property.

Some prior owners were Sidney Saucier, Azoline Saucier, Wilson Arnold, Alan Arnold

503   1895

This is a picturesquely massed two-story frame dwelling with a projecting stepped central pavilion. The double-tiered gallery is set with fluted Tuscan Ionic columns with a turned balustrade on the second level. The full-length four-over-four windows service the gallery. A boxy two-story rear addition was constructed in 1915. Renovations and additions were made in 1986. A white picket fence fronts the property.

Historic Note: It was originally built for the Tessier family. Some prior owners were Martha Bailey, Tessier, Harding, H.H. and Catherine G. Hanson, John Mullen, Tom Currie, William Kornhaus, Riley Stonecipher.

501   1910
Melodia House.
This two-story, frame, Colonial Revival dwelling has an inset gallery and a shed-roofed upper gallery set into the gable roof. It is coupled with Tuscan columns at the gallery. A Chinese trellis balustrade encloses the second level. It was remodeled to a six bedroom and five bathroom menage.
Some prior owners were James Gaudet, Henry Ritayik, Joseph A. Percy, Joseph Airey, James Lake, Michael Eubanks, C.T. Hardie.

Special Note: A former Presbyterian Church was built across the street from the Melodia House.

SEAL AVENUE -- was named for Roderick Seal, former Harrison County Clerk of Court and Sheriff. *Historic Note:* This street was originally called *Hogs Alley*. At the intersection of Seal and Second streets was the largest Live Oak along the Coast which was known as the "King of Oaks." It died in the 1940s. *Historic Note:* On the South of Seal Avenue was located the famed Presbyterian Church which was destroyed by the Hurricane of 1915. Its usable parts, including the bell, pulpit, and some stained window glasses, were moved to the Pineville area on Menge Avenue and has since been known as the Pineville Presbyterian Church. *Historic Note:* The first Pass Water Main was installed from Beach Avenue to Second Street along Seal Avenue. *Historic Note:* Seal Avenue was the most western street within the original Charles Asmard (freed Negro slave) Tract. At the foot of Seal Ave. was a rare tree that was brought in by barge in the 1920s from South America. In the 1950s, citizen ire was raised when the Highway Department wanted to cut down the tree. However, it wasn't cut, resulting in Seal having a crooked turn-off to the highway. Needless to say, in 1995, a work crew cut it down.

113 Seal Avenue
1920
    This one-story, frame, hip-roof cottage has bungaloid detailing with an inset gallery supported by battered pylons on high brick pedestals. It has exposed rafter ends and is a good example of bungaloid detailing that was a common cottage form.

117 Seal Avenue
1895
This is a modest, one-story, frame, hip-roofed, four-bay cottage with an inset gallery. It has double entrance doors that are flanked by six-over-six windows. The home is a good example of the popular coastal vernacular cottage form.

121 Seal Avenue
1910
This is a one-story frame hip-roofed cottage with coupled fenestration and exposed rafter ends. The entrance hood is supported by earlier mill-worked brackets.

123 Seal Avenue
1905

This modest, one-story, frame, hip-roofed cottage has an inset gallery. An older, late-nineteenth-century structure or wing is attached to its rear. It was extensively remodeled with new materials, with careful preservation of its original massing.

127 Seal Avenue
1900
Kiskadee

This modest, one-story, frame, hip-roofed, four-bay cottage has an inset gallery supported by simple gallery posts with stepped caps. The coupled entrance doors are flanked by six-over-six windows. The structure's facade is set with flush siding. It is the best preserved structure of the row of dwellings.

131 Seal Avenue
1900
This is a typical, one-story, frame, hip-roofed vernacular cottage with an inset gallery supported by plain gallery posts with molded caps and an X-motif balustrade. It is a good example of the popular coastal cottage form.

A large side porch addition was made on Second Street giving the cottage greater depth perception.

427*   1890
This picturesquely massed, detailed story-and-a-half dwelling has a steep broad jerkin head roof. The five-bay inset gallery on the first level is balanced by a three-bay second-level gallery set into the roof. It is matched at the rear by a range of French doors to a shallow balcony. Decorative scalloped skirts are elaborated on all eaves. A Porte-cochere is on either side of the gallery. A rear service ell is connected to the house by a frame hyphen. The home was built for D.E. McDonald by builder Frank Wittmann. Some prior owners were D.E. McDonald, Dallis and Julia Rae Ward, Shelia Rafferty Maginis, M.H.

Utley, Leslie and Dorothy Clark, Presilla Clark,.
* McDonald Oaks.

425   1910

This interestingly massed story-and-a-half Colonial Revival dwelling has a jerkin head roof and a second level double-tiered gallery cut into its roof. It is sheltered by a shed roof. The first level five-bay inset gallery has square columns.

Some prior owners were T.V. Courtenay, Warren Bashe, Gulf Plaza Apartments, Lucien Voorhies, Albert Burguieres, H.J. Clark, Capt. Donald DeMetz, Jr.

419   1910

Barksdale House.
This is a handsomely proportioned and detailed, two-story, frame, hip-roofed, Colonial Revival dwelling with matching end solaria. The pedimented entrance hood is carried on slender Tuscan columns. This is an early example of academic Colonial Revival style. The home sports six sun porches. The huge downstairs living room features a fireplace, glassed sun-porch and a screened room across the rear. A circular staircase rises to the four bedroom second level. It was built by Frank Wittmann for Dr. Strong who sold to Luther Barksdale, famous for racing his motorcycle across the Bay St. Louis railroad bridge moments before the oncoming train. Some prior owners were Dr. James Nix, Dr. Carter, M. Bohn, George Wogan, Michael Eubanks.

415   1890

Rest Haven.

This boxy, two-story, frame, vernacular dwelling has a set gable end to street. The double-tiered gallery with an octagonal end on first level, features earlier Eastlake-style millwork on the second level and Colonial Revival, coupled Tuscan columns, on the first level. The balcony with exterior staircase and exterior end chimney on east elevation was replaced after a fire in 1975.

Some prior owners were Esther Cronovich and her sister, Marie Hammerbach, Dr. Earl Saucier, R.L. Simpson, Youban, Hal Wetherby. The Sauciers remodeled the home and had the two-story cottage moved to its present location. *Historic Note:* In 1936, Esther Cronovich operated the home as a ten-room hotel rest home and named the *Rest Haven.* Later owners named it *"High Oaks."*

Historic Note: Reportedly, a (FWC) free-woman of color, had a house at this site which is indicated by piers beneath the present home. It has been recounted that she owned a large tract of land fronting the Beach at this site. Research of early deeds and assessment rolls would suggest that this may have been Rosalie Benoit.

413   1900

Soria-Law House. Win-Rush.

This handsomely proportioned, raised, one-story, frame, hip-roofed dwelling has bungaloid and Colonial Revival styling. The inset gallery is supported by coupled Tuscan columns. The central entrance bay is set with a broad, circular-headed frontispiece surrounding French doors and corresponding side lights, which can be opened. It has a single bungaloid dormer. The commodious central hall, double-pile plan interior with Colonial Revival mantels was

built by builder Frank Wittmann. Some prior owners were former Congressman Paul Maloney, C. Sturgill, Mrs. Ethel A. Hardie, Thomas Adams, H. Cronovich, Marvin Law, James and Pat Mowry. A white picket fence fronts the property.

403   1890   This picturesquely massed, two-story, frame dwelling was constructed with a deep three-bay-wide central pavilion. The hip-roofed gallery wraps around three sides of the house which is set with slender fluted Doric columns and richly detailed with bracketed eaves and a shingled upper level. It has operable louvered blinds.

Some prior owners were Lucille and Irene Weston, W.A. Walsingham, Judge Jim Comiskey, H.W. Griffon.

401   1876
The Rhodes Store.
VFW Hall since 1958 until purchased as the *Palace at the Pass.* This altered two-story frame commercial structure is built to the street with a double-tiered gallery, now set with iron members. The western section has a gambrel roof with pedimented dormers. The eastern section has a hip roof. Parapet originally screened roof ends. It has a unique Eastlake-style oriel window on the second level of its eastern elevation.

Historic Note: The building was originally a shed which became enclosed in 1852. In 1876, C.M. Rhodes, a former mayor, acquired it and greatly expanded it for his business and named it the *Trade Palace* which housed out-of-towners including their horses and ox-teams. Traveling salesmen and farmers brought their wares and produce from inland villages as far away as 120 miles taking up to six weeks traveling time. They came to sell to the locals or to off-shore schooners from the wharfs.

Near this site was an early road which led northeasterly to cross Johnson Bayou to Cuevas, or Pineville, as it is now called. The road was later closed and a new one was cut at Menge Avenue. Cart-rail tracks still beneath the building led out to a wharf into the Sound. In 1902, it was owned by Chapotel, a plumber and builder of several homes on the Coast.
Some other prior owners or tenants included Adolph Bourdin, Frank Wharton, Merchant Marine Warehouse. Then the Palace at the Pass with major renovations to the interior.

FLEITAS AVENUE Named for the Fleitas family headed by Bartholemew Fleitas.

WAR MEMORIAL PARK
Behind the Victorian-styled Gazebo is a tree lined walk-way with 13 Majestic Live Oaks. At dusk,

a panorama of lights shine upward into the tall languishing branches and shine downward in a display of enchanting shadows. Visitors are encouraged to stroll through the walkway path to visit the gazebo -- the veteran and Camille monuments -- and the Presidential towering arboriculture.

Historic Note: Before it was a park, the property was bought by the Widow Simon Cucullu, in 1834, from freed slave, Charles Asmard. The widow built a magnificent mansion which fronted the Live Oaks with a view to the beach. Her daughter, Marie Modeste Dorothee, married Bartholemew Fleitas. She inherited the home and lived there. In 1892, it was sold to John Towle and the following year to Bill Coleman, and then bought by Fred Green, all of Chicago. In 1899, the house, then named *Oak Villa,* was bought by George A. Wiegand who sold it to Albert Aschaffenberg, who owned the Mexican Gulf Hotel that burned down in 1917. The house was torn down prior to the hotel burning in anticipation of expanding the hotel site.

* Presidential Oaks Group

323   (ca 1930)
Caretakers House
This modest, hip-roofed, two-bay-by-two-bay cottage with inset gallery (enclosed) with a rear-ell which was added..

Historic Note: Robert Newman bought the former Fleitas property from Canal Bank of New Orleans, successors after Aschaffenberg's death. In anticipation of building a large residence, he immediately built the small cottage, only to withdraw his option to purchase. After the park grounds were purchased by the Pass Christian War Memorial Park Association, which was initiated by William V. Robinson, the cottage was moved and occupied by Mrs. Marguerite Taconi, the first park custodian. This house was razed in 1999 with no objections by Preservation interests in the community.

319   1875

Bien-Aime.
This unusually massed, one-story, frame, hip-roofed cottage has an attached shed-roofed gallery. The board-and-batten sheathed rear ell is attached to the main house by a small frame hyphen. It was restored and renovated in 1990. *Historic Note:* This sea-side cottage was built for the R.W. Bielenberg family.
Special Note: On the beach side, across from the Park

was the late 1890s, three-story NOLA Apartment building which was razed in 1952 to allow passage-way for U.S. Highway 90.
Prior owners: L. Bielenberg, Barbara Scott.

317   1895

Pernambuco House.
This one-story frame, hip-roofed cottage has a 3-bay, inset gallery. The stylized Tuscan columns carry a simple entablature that continues around the house.

Some prior owners were Frank French, George Morse, Howard Peabody, L.H. Dufrechoe, D.W. Steppic, Belleville Whitehead, Wentworth Horned, Richard Darby, Betty Fowler.

Special Note: three houses, 309, 313, and 317, were moved to their present locations after the Mexican Gulf Hotel had burned in 1917.

313   1890

Bidwell Adam House.
This one-story frame vernacular cottage has an inset gallery. It follows the typical two-room plan with a central interior chimney. The pergola-like porte-cochere and side porch were added after 1930.
Historic Note: This cottage formerly belonged to the Mexican Gulf Hotel. It was built by Clausel Courtenay and

was the residence of Bidwell Adam, a former Lieutenant Governor of Mississippi. Some prior owners were Virginia Seither, Dr. Robert Stewart, Brig. Gen. Howard Haines.

309   1890

This neatly proportioned and detailed one-story, frame, five-bay, Colonial Revival dwelling has a three-bay pedimented portico which is set against its inset gallery supported by quare columns with molded caps. Its is a good example of early local form which continued through the early twentieth century.
Historic Note: The house was originally one of the cottages

belonging to the Mexican Gulf Hotel and has been moved twice.

305*   1925
Bielenberg House.
This is a one-story, five-bay, gable-roofed, bungalow-style dwelling. It has a flat-roofed gallery with plain, square, brick piers that shelters the facade. It was built on the site of the former Mexican Gulf Hotel.

 Some prior owners or tenants were Frank French, Katie Bielenberg,

*Bielenberg & Mexican Gulf Group

DAVIS AVENUE

Davis Avenue was named for Benjamin Davis who purchased the property on the east side of the street in 1853. He was a former member of the Harrison County Board of Police.
Historic Note: Located at the foot of Davis Avenue was the Municipal Pier which extended out into the Sound. A large Pavilion was constructed at its end which not only permitted fishing, crabbing, and shrimping, but also was the scene for many social functions, including parties and dances.

113 Davis Avenue   1905
 This is a diminutive, one-story, stuccoed, Neo-Classical, commercial structure. It has an inset, Tuscan-columned portico and a parapet which conceals a nearly flat roof. The architectural form structure is unaltered.
Historic Note: It was originally built as Hancock Bank's first branch outlet (1905-1928) after having moved from its earlier location in the Northrop Building. It is currently leased out as a professional office building.

265   1928

Hancock Bank.

This monumental, two-story, Beaux Artes, commercial structure of blond brick and sandstone facade is detailed with Corinthian columns in antis carrying entablature and a decorative parapet. Clustered one-over-one sash windows are imbedded on its east elevation. It has a monolithic brick addition to its western side. The interior retains most of its original detailing, including decorative ceiling plaster work, marble banking counter, and a vault frontispiece. *Historic Note:* This was the prior site of the Elmer Northrop Building from 1902 to 1905. It then became the *Idlewald Hotel* which was

acquired by George Taylor who converted the hotel to provide for the Hancock Bank branch office in addition to merchants shops and professional offices. From 1905 to 1928 the Hancock County Bank was housed in its new building to the rear and north of its present location. The current building was built in 1928, where the bank branch office has remained. This building was renovated in 1963 and expanded when the bank purchased the Nelson Hotel next door, providing for drive-up services and the remaining half serves as the Bank Annex building which is also rented out to tenants.

263   1925   – *Nelson Hotel.*

"Hancock Bank Annex" This large, two-story, brick, flat-roofed structure incorporates an earlier two-story garage. It has stepped massing and utilitarian styling with twelve-over-one sash of varying sizes throughout. *Historic Note:* It operated as a hotel from 1925 until 1975. The Hancock Bank renovated the hotel in 1981 by demolishing half of it as a banking drive-through and putting a brand new face on its front including the decorative columns. It underwent additional renovations in 1998. The locals humorously refer to it as the *Half-Nelson.* Its previous owner was Margaret Nelson. The *Annex* is currently leased out as a professional office building.

Some prior owners or tenants included Ware's Auto Garage, Oak Lawn Inn, Andrew and Margaret Nelson, Nelson Beauty Shop, Frank Wharton, Dr. William Neal,

243   1840s *Saucier-Pratt House.*
"Union Quarters" This
impressive, two-story, frame,
double-pile, Greek Revival dwelling
is distinguished by a one-bay
pedimented portico set against the
inset gallery. It has a distinguished
cast-iron filigree balustrade. The
dining room, solarium, and porte-
cochere were added in 1910. It has
a separate octagonal Garconniere
that was built in 1890. A cast iron
fence fronts the property. Profound
renovations and restorations have
been made during the mid to late
1990s, with an emphasis on preservation.

Historical Note: The home was built by Pierre
Saucier, who had 14 children, one of whom was
Anatol Joseph Saucier who married Mary Toulme
of Bay St. Louis. During the Civil War, in April
1862, the Federal troops landed at Pass Christian
and following the war, during the Reconstruction
Period, Federal officers were billeted at the Saucier
Home. Legend has it that Mary had hidden her
infant son Anatol Paul Saucier in the attic until she

was able to determine that the Federal Troops were friendly. As she was playing piano for the
troops one evening, she played the "Bonnie Blue Flag" which was considered a Rebel battle tune.
The young baby, Anatol Paul, grew up to become Alderman, Mayor, and Police Chief of Pass
Christian during the early 1900s. *Historic Marker* reads - *"Union officers were temporarily
quartered here during the invasion of Pass Christian."*
In 1835, Freed Slave Charles Asmard gave his slave, Winny, her freedom and a 200-foot-lot with a
house. Pierre Saucier bought the lot and house in 1841.
On Nov 1, 1871, the "heirs of the Estate of Pierre Saucier" sold the spacious Saucier manor to
Mary Caroline Dewees for $4000.
On October 29, 1885 she sold the beautiful mansion to Louisa Jane Bidwell of New Orleans, who
also increased the size of the mansion and added the octagonal garconniere. An 1896 photo of the
house is shown here.

In June 1900, Dr. George Pratt took full possession of the house and even further enhanced
it in 1910, with a new dining room, a solarium, and a porte-cochere.

In March of 1944, Frank Wharton and his wife's aunt, Mrs. Margaret L. McGrath, jointly
purchased the Union Quarters property. In 1969, the home suffered severe roof damages due to
Hurricane Camille and repairs were made. The Hoffmanns, current owners since 1995, have been
restoring the mansion to its former magnificence with determined deference to architectural form
and heritage craftsmanship.

233   1875
Saucier Cottage.
This is a typical story-and-a-half, four-bay, frame cottage with an inset gallery supported by square columns. The house, which is set back, was built by the Saucier family. During the Civil War and the Reconstruction era it

was lived in by members of the Saucier family. The last reported resident was Mrs. Belle Christovich who died in 1969 at the age of 97. Since then, it has remained vacant and deteriorating. *Early site ownership:* As part of the Charles Asmard Tract, this lot was sold to John V. Dedeaux in 1838, who sold it to John V. Toulme, who in turn sold it to Pierre Saucier in 1843.

225   1849
Knost House.
"Asmard."
This house was originally a one-story two-room cottage with inset gallery and nogging construction. The interior has box fireplaces with plain Grecian mantels in the original rooms.
      Various enlargements were made through the years. In 1845, two rooms were added on the east. In

the 1850s, a partition between two rooms was removed making it one large room. It was enlarged again in 1890, with an addition at the northeast section. Its interior has high cypress beamed ceilings and wide board floors polished by time. *Historical Note:* John William Frederick Knost, an emigrant from Prussia, arrived through New Orleans, claimed title to the house in February 1845. A son, John Henry and Rose M. Knost reared 11 children in the family home. Knost Family tradition claims the original Asmard house was inhabited in the year 1794. This area was part of the Charlot Asmard claim as deeded to him from his slave-holding mistress, the Widow Asmar. Existing documented deeds show that the site was owned during the early 1840s, by Thomas Batson, then Francis Casanova in 1845, and then by his brother-in-law John Victor Toulme before being purchased by John Knost in 1857.

221   1849
Town Library.

This early one-story four-bay, frame cottage was originally built at the front of the street. It has an inset gallery and sheltering sidewalk. The front portion appears to have been built in two sections. The building is empty and not protected from weather and ageing destruction.

Historic Note: The Library was established in 1893, making it the first library

along the Coast between Mobile and New Orleans. The first Association president was Mrs. Isabell Finley. Nanny Sutter operated a school in one side of the building in early 1900s. The building and property were bought in 1905. The house and property which extended from the Gulf to Bayou Portage, was originally owned by the Jebens Family since 1855, and previously by Adelaid Piernas, "FWC," daughter of Joseph Labat, Sr., "FMC," heir of Charles Asmard. When it was acquired in 1905, it was moved from the street front to its present location by the *Ladies Library Association.* The original purchase included Gulf frontage and went rearward to the Bayou Portage marshes.

219   1880

This long, narrow, one-story, frame, shotgun-form, vernacular dwelling has a set gable end to the street. It was built as a typical rental cottage.

Pass Christian had many such rental cottages constructed during the period of 1870 to 1900, that were later destroyed by calamity are razed for newer, more elegant structures.

This well preserved unit sets a good example in heritage preservation.

Some previous owners or tenants included Mrs. Marie

Brown, Joseph Brandt, R.P. McKay, Sr., *Sea Side Studio* in 1985.

213   1920
Allen Building.

Constructed by Charles Thornton, this one-story brick, flat-roofed, commercial building was built on the edge of the street. Its facade is distinguished by a stepped parapet. In 1970, following Camille, the building was remodeled with plate-glass windows and a pent roof.

Historic Note: The structure was originally built as the town post office. It later housed a grocery store, a produce store, dental offices, and an antique shop, prior to its present use as an appliance store.

Some former owners or tenants were N.B. Namias, Jules Roux, Monteleon Grocery, Sinopoli Fruit Stand, Russo Vegetables, Der. Edward Gamard, Dr. Harvey Reese, Dr. George Powers, Phil Ambler Antiques, Thomas Stickland, the Beach Club, and R.R. Allen Electric since 1969.

207   1947
Bohn Building.
"Hillyer House."

This boxy, two-story, frame, commercial-residential duplex was built to the street by owner Edgar Bohn. The Bohn family came to the Pass from Prussia in 1860, with Nicholas Bohn as the Patriarch. His sons were Henry, a shoe merchant and W.J., a blacksmith.

The Hillyer House is operated by a mother and daughter team with select choices of exquisite art-crafts.

203   1910
Lang Building.
"Pass Christian Historical Society Building." This one-story, stuccoed-and-scored-brick, Neo-Classical, commercial structure has a portico in antis. The parapet set above overhanging modillioned cornice hides its flat roof. Its three-bay facade provides a side entrance to rear offices and its central, double-leaf door accesses the former tile-floored banking room.

Historic Note: The building was originally built for the Bank of Pass Christian. It followed as the E.A. Lang Insurance and Realty Co., and was acquired in 1988, by the Pass Christian Historic Society. In 1998, the building mortgage was paid off and in 1999, the building was refreshed. The interior concrete vault with steel door maintains storage for archives of Pass history. Other owners or tenants were A.W. Boggs Insurance, Dr. Wesley Lake, Gulfport Laundry, Dr. George Byrne, International Paper, the Harbor Shop, Land's End,

ST. PAUL AVENUE

Historic Note: The first mission church was built in 1844 lasting just a few years. This was followed by a new (second) St. Paul's Church that was erected in 1851, at a new site, but destroyed by fire in 1876. A new (third) church was built by Father Georget in 1879, which was damaged by Hurricane Camille and the new church was erected in 1970. The *Guadalupe Shrine,* located at the eastern front of the church, is the first of its kind in Southeastern United States. It is a likeness of the vision origination of *Our Lady of Guadalupe* in Tepeyac, Mexico.

Historic Note: St. Mary's College for boys was opened by the Christian Brothers in 1866 and was closed in 1875. A school for girls was opened in 1868, and turned over to the Sisters of Mercy in 1870. In 1882. The boys and girls were combined into one school in 1892, and called St. Joseph's. In 1903, St. Paul's Hall was added and expanded in 1925, with the cornerstone for a brick building laid in 1929. In 1963 the school name was changed to St. Paul.

Special Note. In earlier years, Historic Markers were in greater numbers throughout the Pass. Some were knocked down by Hurricane Camille or picked up by the Mississippi Department of Archives because wording was not accurately stated or supported by fact. The few remaining have been preserved from misappropriation. Of existing markers, three are located along Scenic Drive and two are on Highway 90. The Tricentennial Committee raised funds to install four new Historic Markers with plans for them to be planted by the year 2000.

125   1885
Adam House.
"Inn at the Pass"
Originally known as the
"Artesian Cottage," it
was built by Nicholas
Butchert as a one-story,
frame, hip-roofed cottage
with an inset-gallery. It
was enlarged to two
stories with a boxy full-
length addition that once
featured a picturesquely
detailed gabled end. It
was adorned with detailed
millwork on gallery and it
was one of the first
dwellings to install inside
plumbing with running

water from an artesian well. Extensive 1995 renovations and remodeling converted the home into
a Bed & Breakfast.
Historic Note: E.J. Adam was Editor of the Coast Beacon Newspaper. (1895-1925). He also
served as a U.S. Marshall, Alderman, Mayor, Member of Board of Supervisors, Board of Trustees
of Perkinston and Alcorn colleges. Nicholas Butchert and his cousin, John Butchert, early owners,
were both members of the City council.

121   1905
Taylor & Taylor Realtors.
This is a set back, long,
one-story, frame, hip-
roofed, shotgun-form
dwelling with an inset
gallery. It is distinguished
by its side-hall plan.
Historic Note: This house
is a surviving member of a
pair of structures built to
house workers of the local
seafood-canning factory
which existed in the harbor
where the Yacht Club now
is located.
    Former owners
were Charles and Matield
Wood.

115   1930

The *Exchange Building,* until recently, was called the "Rafferty Building" or the "Heritage Building."

The structure is a is a two-story, stuccoed, brick, commercial, row structure with four separate storefronts and common access to the second level. French doors service new iron balcony carried by plain iron poles. Its facade was extensively reworked after Hurricane Camille. Mervyn S. Rafferty was the original owner of the commercial office building.

In 1998, it was completely restored and refurbished to its original design by the present owner.

Some former owners or tenants included Dr. Donald Rafferty, Bernard Knost Construction, MS Power and Light, WPA Sewing Room, United Gas Corp., Dr. Hebert-Dentist, Mrs. Lillian Phillips, Bish Mathis Institue, Hanson Hardware, Barrons Beauty Shop, Plantation Restaurant, Heritage Investments, C.R. Jones-Attorney, W.L. Holcomb, John Mykolyk, Julian Byrne III, Scenic Street Cafe, Southern Personal Resource, Harbor Shop, Dr. D.J. Kinol, Bahia Shoppe, Videos from the Pass, The Banning Group,

In 1944, the WPA had installed a 70-foot-long aluminum arrow on top of the building.

111*   1936

The *Avalon Theater* building was built by G.A. Schmidt. It is a two-story, stuccoed, brick, commercial structure with a stepped parapet facade. A flat-roofed balcony shelters the sidewalk. An undistinguished brick storefront was added to the first level following Hurricane Camille damages, when it was converted to a commercial office building.

Some prior owners or tenants included H. Dedeaux, The Waterway Co., Tony Pedone's Restaurant, Saigon Restaurant,

Rainbow Pages, Donald & Rose Attorneys, Douglas Ainsworth, DDSI Defense Systems, Ameri-Mex Wholesale Beer, Gulf Coast Breeders, Triton Systems, E.S.I. Corp, Derouen & Webb, Alexander Gedrich,

*Slowe Oak and Jill Joe Oak.

107   1920
Lazar-Griffon Building.
    This one-story brick commercial structure was originally built as a duplex with central chamfered entrances. It was extensively remodeled after damages by Hurricane Camille in 1969, with board-and-batten added to the pseudo-Colonial facade. *Historic Note:* It was originally the Lazar Pharmacy and in 1950, became the Griffon Pharmacy.

101   1890
Adolph Bourdin Building.
This picturesque, one-story, frame, hip-roofed, commercial structure has a chamfered entrance with inset galleries that shelters the sidewalk on its southern and western elevations. It is distinguished by its early four-light with transom storefront windows. As one of the original commercial sites, it stood two stories high with rooms over the sidewalk overhang.

Historic Note: In 1913, President Woodrow Wilson purchased a mullet cast-net from this site, when it was Farrell's General Store. This corner site was first owned by a Free Woman of Color, Celeste Ladner, a grand-daughter of Nicholas Christian d'Ladnier. Her 1835, ownership was derived from the Charlot Asmard Will. In 1854, she sold a 35-foot strip of land to provide for Market Street.
    Some former owners or tenants included Western Union, Ships Gallery, Book Boat, –

MARKET STREET – Divides East from West. The *Pass* has an unusually unique street addressing system. The blocks on each side of Market begin with 100 with a direction of 100 East and 100 West. Further confusion for the newcomer is that on the East, the street numbers on the North side are odd, whereas on the West, the street numbers on the North side are even. Likewise, the South side is odd on the West – and the South side is even on the East. *Historic Note:* Since the 1820s, the center of Town has been at this intersection. In 1838, and again in 1877, the central business section burned down. The Town's earlier City Hall, built in 1927, was an imposing two-story brick building with four large Doric columns facing North from the South side of Scenic Drive at the foot of Market Street. It was demolished after Camille's destruction.

110 West   1920s
Courtenay House
This is a large boxy two-story, stuccoed, hip-roofed, mission-style dwelling. It has a three-bay double-tiered stilted-arcade, with an inset gallery that dominates the facade with cast iron balustrade. It has coupled windows on the side elevations.

It has remained primarily vacant – lending to demolishment by negligence. Some former owners were Drucilla Courtenay, Justin Courtenay,
Historic Note: In 1831, most of the 100 block west of Market Street was originally acquired by Orleanian John Hewlett from U.S. Senator Edward Livingston, then of New Orleans.

116 West
Not Listed - Undated
This picturesque, two-story, brick, Colonial Revival, gable-roofed dwelling has two pedimented dormers with casement windows. The five-bay, square columns, inset gallery with outdoor stairway was built in 1992, as a combination commercial and residential structure. It is unusual in many respects, as a commercial dwelling with architectural design favoring the Tullis-Toledano house in Biloxi. It is nicely

proportioned to compliment the neighborhood with a white picket fence that fronts property.
A former owner of the original home site was Catherine Fitzpatrick.

116 ½ West (118 ½)   1870s

This site has a rear building that is a typical, one-story, gable-roofed, two-room frame cottage with an inset gallery. It has a double-leaf entrance door to each room. In 1958, the house was moved from its original location off Barkley Drive and Beach Boulevard on lands formerly owned by Tschopick.

Special Note: Access is from Second Street, or through the driveway of 116 W. Scenic.

120 West   1850

Blue Rose

This was originally a story-and-a-half, frame, five-bay, coastal cottage; gallery with square columns wrapped around three full sides of the house. Consoles carry the overhanging cornices over each bay on the stuccoed facade. The distinctive pilastered dormers were added. The galleries were enclosed with glass for commercial design. Ells are attached to the rear outbuilding. A cast iron fence fronts property. Originally, the home belonged to the Hugh

Fitzpatrick family who were active in Pass community affairs: Miss Katie was appointed Postmaster in 1937; Mrs. Elena was the Chamber of Commerce Secretary, Deputy Clerk and Tax Collector for the City, and Sister Mary Camillus was with the Sisters of Mary Order.

Historic Note: The National Trust for Historic Preservation has described it as, "the most significant antebellum house on the western portion of Pass Christian's beachfront. **Special Interest:** Each prior and current owner have their own special experiences about the ghostly apparitions which are said to haunt this house. A Former Restaurateur, Binh Ly, dug up 150 Scottish-English ale bottles dating from 1830 through 1890 that were used as a walk-way between the two large palm trees in the front yard. *Also, of note:* Another Restaurateur, operating as "La Galarie", was Paul Mattox who was cast in several TV commercials, one of which, was the *Marlboro Man.* Prior to being a restaurant, it was the home of Mrs. Hugh Fitzpatrick who was one of the daughters of Mrs. Manders who affected the famous *"Bedsheet Surrender"* as the Federal Troops were shelling the Town in April 1862. Mrs. Manders home was located on the south side of Scenic prior to Highway 90 being constructed. This was more recently known as the *Blue Rose Restaurant* and its current owners have extensively and majestically remodeled the interior two levels.

122 West   1860
This two-story, frame, gable-roofed, coastal cottage has a double-tiered inset gallery with giant-order square columns. It is considered a good example of this regional vernacular form. It has accordion-style upper-level banisters and is fronted by a cast-iron fence. It is a commercial residence operating as the *Evangeline*. *Historic Note:* This building was incorporated into the Crescent Hotel complex during the 1880s. One of the former owners was Andrew Stewart.

126 West   1860
The *Crescent Hotel*. Later, the "Harbour Inn Bed & Breakfast." The large, two-and-a-half-story, frame, gable-roofed, coastal cottage has double-tiered inset galleries with clapboard siding. Pedimented dormers protrude from the roof line. Following Camille hurricane, it was temporary quarters for the Pass Christian Yacht Club. *Historic Note:* This is the only extant 19th century structure built as a hotel in Pass Christian. Constructed by Patrick

Curtis, it was originally called the *Live Oak House*. In 1888, William Hart acquired it and operated the Crescent Hotel with his three sisters, Miss Mollie, Miss Nellie, and Miss Julia. Charles Dyer's *Along the Gulf* states, "this was one of the best known hostelries . . . everything used in the shape of poultry, eggs, butter, milk, vegetables, fruit, etc., is raised on the farm in the rear of the estate."

 Since 1991, much of the early traditions are carried forth by owners, Diane and Tony Brugger, who made extensive restorations in 1998. Some former owners included Mae McDonald, M. Dambourian, Margaret Duval, Durell Grosch, Sara Beggs, Robert Campbell, Vince Campbell, William Barrett, Diane and Tony Bruger.

 Historic Note: John L. Sullivan stayed at the hotel while he was training for the fight at Mississippi City on February 7, 1882. That was the last bare knuckle bout and Ryan was knocked out in the 9th round.

 Special Note: The Pass Christian Yacht Club had their club facilities on the beach side of the hotel – it was torn down in 1952. Other prior names for the Hotel were the *Lido* and the *Meadow House*.

128 West   1885
This one-story, frame, Queen Anne cottage has a broad, gable-roofed, pavilion which features an octagonal end and a bay window. *Historic Note:* Mrs. Jane Northrop operated this home as *"Jane's Praline Kitchen"* from 1918 to 1942.

Some prior owners or tenants of this property were Jane Northrop, Byrne & Rick Realty, Sandpiper, Dr. D.J. Inkol.

130 West   1890
Unaltered, this one-story, frame, hip-roofed, coastal cottage has an inset gallery with square columns. It has denticulated cornice and an octagonal-ended bay centered on its rear elevation. This is a good example of the popular regional vernacular form.

Some prior owners or tenants included Walter, Mae, and Alma McDonald.

134 West   1890

This is a richly detailed and picturesquely massed, story-and-a-half, frame, Queen Anne cottage. The gallery features turned posts with spool frieze and corner brackets. It is adorned with gable pieces and an eastlake frontispiece. It is the best example of Queen Anne style in the district.

Some prior owners were William Desposito, Donald DeMetz, Charles DeMetz,

136* West   1925
Lang House.
This story-and-a-half, frame, gable-roofed bungalow has an inset gallery supported by coupled square columns. A geometric lattice screen links the columns. Centered shed-roofed dormer. One of the most exemplary bungalows in the district. *Historic Note:* At this site was the home of Miss C.A. Hiern, daughter of Finley Hiern, the town's

first mayor and second Lighthouse Keeper, and after him, was appointed the Lighthouse Keeper from 1844 to 1861. She was also the town's Postmistress.

Some other owners were E.A. Lang, L.W. Alston,

* Lang Oak, 440 years old.

HIERN AVENUE

Hiern Avenue was probably named for the entire Hiern family. Roger Alden Hiern was one of the original sales agents promoting land sales and constructed the lighthouse in 1831. Finley Bottm Hiern was the first mayor of Pass Christian and the first president of the Harrisson County Board of Police, Cornelia Hiern bought one of the first lots from Edward Livingston along with her husband, Charles Shipman, and Miss Catherine Hiern was the lighthouse keeper from 1844 to 1861.

200 West
Not listed – Undated
City Hall.
This one-story, blond-brick, flat-roofed structure with inset galleries front and rear was built in 1970. *Historic Notes:* The first Lighthouse on the Mississippi mainland was erected at this site in 1831. The property was purchased from Edward Livingston in 1830 for $250. Lighthouse keepers were Roger Hiern, Finley Hiern, Catherine Hiern, B.F. Johnson, Laurence Hyland, Marie Reynolds, Sallie Dear. The Light tower was terminated in September 1882 and sold at auction to Lawrence Fallon in April 1883.

This was also the site of the four-story-brick, Pass Christian high school which was built in 1908 and classes were terminated in 1937. The building was used for a number of community and business purposes before being torn down following extensive damages by Hurricane Camille.

The new City Hall was dedicated as a memorial to Hurricane Camille victims; and a time capsule was placed in the front lawn to be opened in the year 2070.

The 1908 corner stone of the old City Hall at Market Street, was placed at the foot of the American Flag pole in front of the Hall.

204 West   ca 1840
The Bourne House.
This is a large, story-and-a-half, frame, gable-roofed, coastal cottage with an inset gallery refreshed in a bungalow style dwelling. It is distinguished by a large pedimented dormer with coupled sash. It was remodeled in 1910.

Historic Note: Deed Book research evidences that the house was apparently built prior to the death of its first owner, Thomas Cabrannel in 1843. Finley B. Hiern acquired it by auction and sold it to John Curran and Ignatious Kriggick, who conveyed his interest to John Curran in 1854. Curran evidently made substantial renovations to the house based on the monetary size of his mortgage. In turn, he left his estate to his sister, Ellen, who sold it to Mary Agnes Hart, who left it upon her death to her sisters, Helen and Julia Hart. Edward and Rowena Bourne acquired it in January 1933.

Special Note: Adlai Stevenson vacationed in this home while attending school in New Orleans.

208 West   1880
Robertson-Lake House.
This is a distinctive, story-and-a-half, frame, clipped-gable-roofed dwelling with richly detailed pedimented dormers. The inset gallery is supported by massive chamfered posts. A small pediment defines the central entrance bay. It is noted for its interesting vertical proportions. It has a rear service ell. The home was restored in the early 1980s. A white picket fence fronts the property.
Historic Note: The house belonged to two well known Pass Christian physicians, Dr. A.R. Robertson in 1892, and Dr. Wesley Lake, during the early 1970s.

Some other prior owners were Amy Richardson, Virginia Hagen, Frank Browne, Richard Yeager, Norris Harris, Charles Richards,

Special Note: Norris Harris was also the owner of *"South Fork,"* the house shown on the TV series, *Dallas.*

226 West   1910

Previously known for an early owner, E. Domingue during the 1940s, it is a story-and-a-half frame dwelling. The gallery is set with Tuscan columns. It has a cast-iron balustrade. The modern dormers intrude on its antebellum integrity. Some other owners were John Baillaux, Dr. W.P. Bradburn, Dr. W. Ellinger, Peter Ferrara.

230 West   1890

Referred to as the *Logan House.* It is a picturesque two-story, frame, mock-mansard-roofed house. The dwelling incorporates an earlier antebellum structure. Some period plaster work survives. Richly detailed gallery with spool frieze. One of the most distinctively styled residences in the district. The home is architecturally unaltered with a rear service ell.

It was previously owned by the Joseph Craven family in the 1930s and later owned by Gabriella B. Logan.

Henderson Avenue

Henderson Avenue was named for John Henderson, Sr.who was part of a combine that bought the Livingston Tract in 1837, consisting of all the peninsula, ranging from the Bay of St. Louis to the middle of Long Beach. The original name for the street was Portage Avenue. Henderson originated from New Jersey, became a lawyer, a state Senator and U.S. Senator from Mississippi. He left a large portion of Pass Christian to his heirs who continued land sales into the 1920s.

520 West   1911
Watkins-Hecht House, also known as *Middlegate.*
Numerous additions. Large, rambling, two-story, frame bungalow continually enlarged since its construction. One-story projecting gabled pavilion set against two-story mass of house creates picturesque massing. *Historic Note*: Extensive, elaborate Japanese gardens, complete with pavilions and statuary, at one time ranked among the finest in the United States. The gardens were developed by Mr. and Mrs. Rudolph Hecht during the years of 1923-1929.

Known as the Middlegate Gardens, many authentic oriental pieces were imported from Japan which included a great bronze Buddha. As a result of Camille damages the Garden is no longer shown to the public.

Historic Note: Wm. Wiegand reported that the nearby Lynne Castle Hotel grounds may have been the gravesite of Indian Chief Moniac, who was presented a medal by General George Washington. A grave was found containing silver ornaments while workmen were digging a well.

Pine Street

Magnolia Street

710 West   1871
The Seagulls
This beautiful home was originally built by the Marks family in 1871. In the 1930s, the McClellan family replaced the first level columns with its brick arches. With sustained damages incurred by Hurricane Camille, it was restored with careful detail to its former appearance.

        It is a richly detailed, raised, one-story, frame dwelling set on a high brick basement. Five-bay facade sheltered by flat-roofed portico on arcaded base. Fluted Corinthian columns, turned balustrade, bracketed cornice that continues on gable ends. Facade set in German siding. Copping on ridge of roof. Architecturally, the home is one of the most distinguished structures in the district. Prior to 1900s, the house was owned by family names such as: Marks, Samuels, Ziporah Carpenter, T.L. Airey, and Raphael Gianella. In the 1900s by William Couturie, Tom Grayson, E. Aschaffenberg, Byron McClellan, Byron Humphries,

716 West   1925
This is a boxy, two-story, frame, hip-roofed Colonial Revival dwelling with a flat-roofed gallery supported by Tuscan columns which wrap around three sides. The present structure incorporates an antebellum dwelling including artful workmanship of beautiful dated moldings and unusual casement windows with jibs. The house extends rearward to St. Louis Street. It was owned by the Thomas Gilmore family of New Orleans from the 1880s to

the 1940s, and later by Felix Vaccaro. Herbert Hanson made major renovations as a result of Camille damages. In the early 1920s, it was the summer dwelling of New Orleans preservationist, Martha Robinson.

Some other owners were G.R. Keating, R.H. Richard,

722 West   1849   1930
Originally this home was a one-story, five-bay, vernacular, Greek Revival dwelling with an inset gallery. In the 1930s, it was raised to its present two stories, with the ground level bricked in. At its rear entranceway, there is a picturesque, unusually massed, two-story, kitchen/cottage outbuilding used as a guest cottage. The home was moved back and turned around from its prior Beach Boulevard location. Some other family owners were: McGinty, Penrose, Sharp, Johnson, Scott, Collins,

Historic Note: John Robert Waterman arrived in the Pass prior to the Civil War and became an early owner of this home, which was later owned by William B. Burkenroad and later by Adele Penrose Sharp.

Cedar Avenue

Named for the large tract of Cedar trees that were once near that location during the early 1800s.

800 West 1909 The Parham-Katz House was earlier called the *Belvedere.* This majestic mansion is a lavishly detailed two-and-a-half-story, frame, Colonial Revival dwelling with a giant-order, flat-roofed portico and end pavilions. The interior plan adds gracious continuity to the home. The house was remodeled circa 1925 by Frank Wittmann. Some prior owners to the property were: Ferdinand Katz, Belvedere, Zetzman, Ben Brown, Carl Anderson,

1010 West 1915 This two-story, frame, three-bay, gambrel-roofed, Colonial Revival dwelling has a large, shed-roofed dormer with coupled sash. It has an inset gallery with Tuscan columns. Sliding glass doors have replaced the original first level windows and some of the lawn area has been displaced with a swimming pool. Some prior owners have been Brounlow Jackson, Jr., John Foster, and John Fitzgerald.

1012 West   1922
The Castle. Numerous additions until 1966 by owners George and Jessie Gundlach. This unique, two-story, eclectic, mission-style dwelling was made of hand poured concrete. It has a stepped parapet and an offset circular tower which dominates the facade. Painted Greek meander string course.

Some prior owners were James Sherman, George and Jessie Gundlach, Donald Kennelly,

1020 West   1923
Woodland Cottage.

This story-and-a-half frame gable -roofed bungalow has a three-bay hip-roofed gallery supported by paneled square columns. It has a prominent, broad, shed-roofed dormer from its roof. In the 1930s, the home was added to with tenderly cared for gardens planted by Mr. and Mrs Charles R. Currie. The home has remained in the family by several

generations of descendants. The home was rendered modifications in 1961, and was expanded by rear additions in 1998, all with strict conformity to its architectural heritage and family pride of workmanship. With an added rear bedroom wing, the main house was refitted with a spacious living room and library in addition to accommodating a grand courtyard contiguous to the dining room. Using an unaltered fireplace as a model, one which had been changed in 1961 was brought back to its original styling.

1024 West   1890
Originally named *Whitehall..*

This is a boxy, two-story, frame, hip-roofed, Colonial Revival dwelling that has a double-tiered inset gallery. Its first level piers are of brick. The second level is set with Tuscan columns and a turned balustrade. The handsome Colonial Revival staircase was installed during the 1950s with refitting by architects Koch and Wilson of New Orleans. *Historic Note*: An on-site small cottage predates the main house possibly to 1840. As reported in Wm. Wiegand notes, this was one of the samples of early dwellings built by John Henderson as part of his lot sale promotions in the Pass. Beams were made of whole young trees and all timbers, including floor boards were pegged together by one of the McDonald craftsmen. Mrs. Grace Jones moved the "ell" from the west cottage to form the east cottage during the 1940s.

Some prior owners or tenants were James Shows, Stanford Morse, and Robert Ewing Brown. *Historic Note:* Miss Rose Stith was librarian at the Town Library in the early 1900s. Family descendants claim that the main house was built in 1870 and was named for the Stith family residence in Virginia.

Special Note: Noted guests of the home were Henry Clay and house tenant, Captain Joseph T. Jones, who built the City of Gulfport and completed the railroad and port facilities there.

1040 West   1923
Casa Blanca, the one-story stuccoed mission-style dwelling has an arcaded gallery and a tile roof. It is picturesquely massed maintaining its integrity. During an earlier period, metal tracks extended from the house running out to its long pier allowing wagons to carry supplies and people to the bath house. Its interior has high ceilings and a number of French doors. Some former owners were: Lewis Carvalho (the Portugese Consul in 1920), Eleanore DelBondio, Marie Bertrand, A.C. Suhren and William Steward.

Glossary of Architectural Terms

Baluster – Small posts that support the upper rail, or railing, as on a staircase.

Bungalow = A low house, usually one-storied, with a wide sweeping porch and sometimes an attic.

Chamfered = Angled or grooved.

Cornice = The molding along the top of a wall or building, or the decorative strip above a window.

Dado = The lower part of wall base when adorned with a facing; or a groove.

Dormer = An upright window or roofed projection in a sloping roof.

Eclectic = Composed of elements drawn from various origins.

Entablature = An upper wall section supported on columns.

Gable = A triangular-shaped wall covered by the ends of a ridged roof.

Garconniere = Servants' Quarters, or sometimes used as bachelor's quarters

Hip roof = A roof with sloping ends and sides.

Modillioned = Ornamental block or bracket under the corona of the cornice.

Nogging = Rough brick masonry used to fill in the open spaces of a wooden frame.

Oriel Window = Large bay window projecting from wall supported by a bracket.

Palladian = Related to a revived classic style in architecture.

Pediment = A low-pitched gable on the front of some buildings

Pedimented = A triangular space forming the gable of a 2-pitched roof in classic architecture or a similar form used as a decoration.

Pergola = An arbor or projecting cover with an open roof of cross rafters.

Pilaster = A rectangular support or pier, like a column, projecting partially from a wall.

Porte-cochere = Roofed structure extending from building over an adjacent driveway. (Car Port)

Portico = A porch or covered walk supported by columns, often projecting over a driveway at the entrance to a building.

Truncated = Cut short or appearing as such.

Tuscan = Of a classical (Roman) order of architecture, marked by smooth columns with a ringlike top and no decorations.

Tympanum = The recessed space enclosed by the slanting cornices of a pediment.

Katrina Remembered

Two days before Katrina, I delivered a Talk on one of my books, "Diamondhead Discovered" to a group assembled at the book store in Diamondhead. Having presented the same talk several times, I barely scanned my notes. My general topics covered the water ways of the Bay St. Louis, the Jourdan River, formerly called St. Germaine by the French, and Baneeshewa, the Indian name for Rotten Bayou, – also pointing out the oldest European House known as Cuevas, and that the nearby communities were the Kiln and Fenton.

During the wrap-up of the book review, questions led to the impending hurricane as predicted to land somewhere West of New Orleans. Some of the gathering stated that they were already packed ready to forage for inland havens, while others stated they were remaining intact. I gave the observation from my book, that the area of Diamondhead was left high and dry, during and after, Hurricane Camille which was the worst storm to hit the area since 1915.

With that thought in mind, I left my home at Pass Christian, Mississippi as a result of a final call by the police to evacuate or else. A friend, Kathleen from Diamondhead, 20 miles inland, had called me earlier, to offer her home there as she had done on a previous hurricane threat.

After minimally securing my house, and having moved my Honda to higher ground, I left in my Ford with my computer, one change of clothes, and my .38.

The night was fine as I slept on the couch in the living room. I awoke early and waited for the TV news to give me an update but the electricity went out about 7:30 a.m. indicating that the winds from the impending hurricane had threatened part of the area. I then went out to my Ford and turned on the radio as the local station stated that the water was rising and the winds had gained strength and the reporter announced that the hurricane was due for a direct hit at Pass Christian and Bay St. Louis at 8:10 a.m. It was then 8:05, so I closed up my car and went inside being trailed by the whooshing of the winds driving on the nearby trees as the rain started seriously to hit the roof.

I lived my own story in that house that became flooded and for fear raised myself to the attic before the water subsided a few hours later. It was then that I began pondering what may have happened in Pass Christian. It wasn't until two days later that I was able to hike a ride to the Pass to see first hand for myself.

In a note book, I had written the following:
August 31, 2005 — Television and pictures could never tell the destruction and first hand sights encountered that day. I listed some of the things witnessed at the Pass. South of the railroad tracks is complete destruction, only a few homes on 2nd Street still standing but with significant damage. The cemetery was uprooted of coffins and tumbled headstones were everywhere. The homes on North street were destroyed, many moved off pilings and sitting in middle of the streets. Downtown businesses and offices were significantly wiped out. All the beach front property was gone as far as could be seen. The Harbor area was littered with cars and debris and Highway 90 was impassable.

It wasn't until the following week that security for Timber Ridge was lifted and I was permitted to reach my house. Not much to salvage. I drove to the West on Hwy 90 and found only three structures remaining at the far end. They were each made of brick and mortar.

I drove to the East and found many destroyed and wondered how many would be able to be rehabilitated and restored.

During the Recovery process, even though I was no longer staying in the Pass, I was most pleased when ever called upon to send documents and photos which I had on file and were able to lend some assistance to Pass Christian residents seeking to make insurance claims or to those who wanted dwelling photographs for their contractors to abide by in making restorations.

All the large file photos that I had taken of Katrina's wrath to Scenic Drive structures were lost due to a disk crash. I thought this only happened to others, not to me. So I am very thankful to Ron Daley who has been "on the scene" on the Gulf Coast so some of his images are also posted in the later part of this book.

Numbers of people have asked me to write a book on Katrina, but found myself unable to push the pen or stroke the keys until most recently. I like many others was more concerned for the losses along Scenic Drive than for the loss of my own home in Timberidge.

So a book, unlike my book on Camille, which covers the whole Gulf Coast of Harrison County destruction and called "All About Camille," – my book on Katrina, "Katrina Remembered," is primarily centered on Pass Christian and the stresses born by the citizens and their climb to Recovery.

Katrina Effect

     This photo shows the second level of my home that was flooded by the effects of a 33 foot high tidal surge that had hit the beaches.

     A view of the toll upon my library where I kept my inventory of books, collection of maps, rare books, and references as well as 12 years of research data in the form of diagrams and hand-written notes transcribed from courthouse archival records.

     However, what was saved, is my computer which I took with me when I evacuated. Copies of my 20 odd books were fortunately saved. This is when I decided to distribute my books on whatever other Computer Media comes along. Thank you for your continued interest in the heritage of the Mississippi Gulf Coast which lost most of its historic buildings, historic markers, and historic mansions on the morning of August 29, 2005.

Dan Ellis
Dan@PassChristian.Net
http://PassChristian.Net

Pass Christian's History of Hurricanes

On the average, the Mississippi Gulf Coast is struck by hurricane-force winds every nine years. These statistics have been derived from the time of the first recorded storm in 1717. These factors do not stop the population growth on the Coast, nor does it cause long-time residents to leave. Residents of the Gulf Coast have a great affinity for their habitat, even more so, at Pass Christian for its heritage.

> *Because of the great loss of life in Pass Christian following Hurricane Camille, the Mississippi State Legislature passed statutes making forced evacuation a law — also new building code constraint laws were passed. Likewise, with Hurricane Katrina, we can expect new statutes as well as new Federal guidelines and new local ordinances.*

Pass Christian's Hurricane Pole

Little known to newcomers and even many long time residents, is the 28-foot pole, above MSL, located at the west-side southern end of the Municipal Harbor. The post registered four hurricane flood tides. Atop the post is a weather measuring device from which WLOX-TV received its weather reporting data. Through the years the post has become heavily rusted and obscures the names of the hurricanes, but steel bands remain to show the tidal surge heights. Camille was marked at 25 feet.

Without an extension, or replacement, the pole cannot show the registration of Hurricane Katrina's 32-foot storm surge.

> *Pass Christian's shoreline has been battered by hurricane winds and storm surge walls of water for hundreds of years. It appears that with continued diminishing of coastal barrier islands, storm surges are progressively more serious and hazardous to loss of life and property.*

WLOX-TV Weather Pole
Pass Harbor Marina

Katrina — August 29, 2005

These were the only structures left standing west of Henderson Ave. in Pass Christian. Both locations were made of concrete.
The bottom, known as Castle Sherman was built in the 1920s. The top two buildings on one site were built in 2004.

400 East Scenic Drive

Fleitas Avenue on the West — Seal Avenue on the East

The 400 block of Front Street, as it was originally called, was historically part of the Charles "Charlot" Asmard Negro slave's ownership. This was the eastern end of his 3900 front footage ownership of mid-town Pass Christian.

401, 403, 413, and 415 East Scenic Drive.

419, 425, and 427 East Scenic Drive.

The Palace in the Pass

The staid and stable 150 year old building underwent a reversed transmogrification by some simplistic but essential alterations and tender care that had been rendered by its new owners, P.J. Hughes and her son, Randy Tuggle. The two, PJ and Randy hah turned a white elephant into a much needed showplace that was offered as a facility for social entertainment much as conducted by the Chapotels for Mardi Gras Balls during the early 1900s and by the VFW following WWII, where dances, bingos, suppers, and private receptions were held for nearly thirty years.

The inside renovations were in elegant taste with the Grand Ballroom reminiscent of the former stately Pass hotels in which Grand Balls were held. In addition, the transformed facility afforded a great adjunct to the annual Park events.

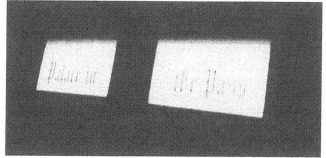

Shadowed images from Sunlight

The Palace was disintegrated into debris, watched over by the damaged house at 403

The owner, P.J. Hughes never had a chance to see the original destruction to her "Palace," which contained many expensive items of European and Early American treasures of furniture and crystal and dishware. The destroyed building was further disintegrated and spread in shambles along Fleitas Avenue by bulldozers that were commissioned to clear all downtown streets.

One of so very many historic places that were listed in the Historic Registry are now gone forever.

427 East Scenic*   circa 1890

This picturesquely massed, detailed story-and-a-half dwelling has a steep broad jerkin head roof. The five-bay inset gallery on the first level is balanced by a three-bay second-level gallery set into the roof. It is matched at the rear by a range of French doors to a shallow balcony. Decorative scalloped skirts are elaborated on all eaves. A Porte-cochere is on either side of the gallery. A rear service ell is connected to the house by a frame hyphen.

    The home was built for D.E. McDonald by builder Frank Wittmann.

    Some prior owners were D.E. McDonald, Dallis and Julia Rae Ward, Shelia Rafferty Maginis, M.H. Utley, Leslie and Dorothy Clark, Presilla Clark,.

* Live Oaks are named McDonald Oaks.

Before and After Profiles from Katrina

Trinity Church

Before Katrina

After Katrina

Exchange Place

2005/11/05

239 East Second St.

Hancock Bank

Palace in the Pass (VFW)

Harbor View Deli

Chamber of Commerce

St. Paul Church

Twin Oaks Lodge

Blue Rose

2005/11/05

Blue Rose

EJ Adam House

Harbour Oaks

Timber Ridge Fairway Dr

12/04/2005

Union Quarters

12/10/2005

Middlegate and the Japanese Gardens were famous since the 1920s

Middlegate -- Main Residence --- ALL GONE

City Hall

Clark and Second St -- Joe Piernas

Warren & Nanette Mueller -- 635 Ponce De Leon -- The Isles

Here is a before and after photo of my house on BeachView in Pass Christian,
The cross street of my house is Everett St that runs alongside the Railroad...
Every house is destroyed to the ground in the BeachVista subdivision. There is not a structure standing.

Before and After at 309 E. Beach Blvd owned by Jeff and Amy Steiner
Along with my brother Charlie Stewart, we stayed during the hurricane. We all survived. Losing the house is very
upsetting -- not only because we just finished renovating the house a year ago, but it is the house I grew up in.
Amy S. Steiner, RN, CPNP, MSN
Director, Clinical Support Services

Katrina ripped apart 80 percent of the homes in Pass Christian. Henderson Point, Pass Christian Isles, Timber Ridge, the West End — were left desolated — battered by the 125 mph winds and crushed by the 32-foot storm surge.

What Katrina took away . . .
Is Being Put Back.
Photos by Ron Daley

Made in the USA
Lexington, KY
15 September 2012